THE *Readied* CHILD

PARENTING TOOLS FOR LEARNING AND LIFE READINESS

Written By

HEIDI TRINGALI, MS, OTR/L

with Ellen Wingate

Illustrated By

GALE WHITMAN

galewhitman.com

Cover By

CHRISTINA GONG

Published by hope*books
2217 Matthews Township Pkwy
Suite D302
Matthews, NC 28105
www.hopebooks.com

hope*books is a division of hope*media

Printed in the United States of America

First paperback edition.
Paperback ISBN: 979-8-89185-458-1
Hardcover ISBN: 979-8-89185-367-6
Ebook ISBN: 979-8-89185-368-3

Library of Congress Number: Application Submitted

All Scripture quotations, unless otherwise indicated, are taken from the Holy Bible, New International Version®, NIV®.
Copyright ©1973, 1978, 1984, 2011 by Biblica, Inc.TM Used by permission of Zondervan. All rights reserved worldwide.
www.zondervan.comThe "NIV" and "New International Version" are trademarks registered in the United States Patent and
Trademark Office by Biblica, Inc.TM

Endorsements

The Readied Child stands apart from other parenting books I've encountered. It offers clear strategies to transform parenting from guesswork to intentional, purposeful practice. The engaging and easy-to-implement tools help parents nurture children's self-regulation, foster accurate self-assessment, and build successful group membership skills. Thoughtful, actionable, and uplifting—this book empowers families to raise regulated, self-aware kids who are able to thrive while participating in life to their fullest.

Judith Coucouvanis
Nurse Practitioner and Author of *Super Skills:*
A Social Skills Group Program for Children with Asperger
Syndrome, High-Functioning Autism and Related Challenges

The first time I read Heidi's words, I knew they needed to become a book to encourage and equip parents everywhere. *The Readied Child* is an exceptional resource for parents who want to intentionally prepare their children for learning and life. Heidi combines research-informed insight with practical, achievable strategies that build both skill and confidence in parents, knowing they're giving their child the best start possible. This isn't a one-time read, but a book parents will refer to repeatedly as they guide their child's early development.

Sharon Jaynes
Best-selling author of 26 books including *The Power of a*
Woman's Words: How the Words You Speak Shape the Lives of Others
and Praying for Your Child from Head to Toe: A 30-Day Guide to
Powerful and Effective Scripture-Based Prayer.

The tools and techniques shared in this book have been incredibly impactful with our son. As we continue to integrate them into our daily lives, we see the positive influence they are having on our entire family. We're so thankful for the new lens Heidi provides in *The Readied Child*!

Brittany and **Taylor Moton,**
Parents and NFL Offensive Tackle, Carolina Panthers

From the moment we met Heidi, our lives changed. Because of *The Readied Child*, we now feel empowered as parents. We have learned new ways to engage with our children and help them become their best selves. Our lives are forever changed in the most incredible ways thanks to T.O.T.S, Heidi, and her novel approach to OT.

Amanda and **Steve Maney,**
Parents and DJ, Kiss95.1, Maney and LauRen Morning Show

This has become one of my new favorite books! From the humor, the practical tips, and the in-your-face reality of why our children are struggling today, *The Readied Child* is quickly becoming my go-to parenting book. I am grateful for Heidi's honesty, compassion, and her ability to offer real-world examples that have changed the trajectory of our family.

Sammy Pandolfo,
Mom and social media influencer, Supporting Chaos

I am a retired special education teacher who specialized in autism. Even more importantly, I am a Nana to a grandson diagnosed with Autism Spectrum Disorder, Level 1. After my grandson's diagnosis, we began searching for the best occupational therapist in the Charlotte, North Carolina area. Heidi Tringali was at the top of the list—and our family quickly realized we had struck gold.

The Readied Child reflects the same thoughtful, compassionate, and highly effective practices that helped my grandson develop greater regulation, confidence, and a stronger sense of connection and capability within his environment. This book reflects Heidi's deep respect for children and families and serves as a reassuring, practical guide for parents and professionals who support individuals requiring occupational therapy services.

Karen A. Newcomb, M.S.Ed
Retired Educator, Mom, and Nana

Dedication

This book is dedicated to every parent who picks it up. May you discover the confidence and courage you have always possessed.

Acknowledgements

Every book needs three things: a best friend, a fight song, and endless access to a beach. Ellen Wingate, this book would not exist without you. Your elegance with the English language, unwavering enthusiasm for this cause, and capacity to remain present even when things get chaotic made you the writing partner I never knew I needed. Your gentle grace with my words was a gift, and your saint-like tolerance of my incessant playing of *"Lion"* by Brandon Lake while I found the courage to write is nothing short of heroic. There will never be a thank you big enough for all that you have done.

Dr. Jan Watkins, you rewrote the course of my life. Sitting in your office at Hastings College, your words guided me to pursue Occupational Therapy, a path I never imagined but now cherish deeply. Because of your wisdom and foresight, I am now able to provide OT services through the lens of an educator. I am inspired by the ways you continue to seek transformation for others.

Sharon Jaynes, my mentor, guide, and voice of encouragement: thank you for believing in me and in this message. Thank you for guiding me along a path that was entirely new and unfamiliar. Thank you for answering my texts, taking my calls, and sharing meals while imparting your wealth of knowledge and experience. Your expertise is matched only by your humility, and I will always strive to write with the integrity and grace that you embody.

Tony, my husband, you are my quiet anchor and most grounded cheerleader. Because of you, I have the freedom to dream, try, fail, and succeed. You give me space and support in equal measure, and your words—though few—are always rational and impactful. Thank you for being steadfast, loving, and unwavering.

Sedonia and Thomas, my children—God knew exactly what He was doing when He placed us together as a family. Sedonia, thank you for walking beside me on this journey with such strength, compassion, and unwavering love. Thomas, thank you for lifting my spirit with your humor, patience, and steady encouragement. Together, you continually challenge me to grow, to love more deeply, and to live more fully. My life is immeasurably richer because of you both.

And to God, who placed these extraordinary people in my life and planted *The Readied Child* in my heart: thank You. You hold our dreams before we can even imagine them and carry us through every step to bring them to life.

Table of Contents

Foreword

by Ellen Wingate

Hearing the words, "We'd like to extend an offer for your son to start TK in the fall," caused my heart to leap. To attend the same school as his dad was incredible, but knowing what a great fit it would be for our oldest child was what caused the tears to form as I reached out to embrace our admissions liaison.

It all sounds so formal, especially for someone who attended public school in a fairly small town. But knowing that a public school setting wasn't going to be ideal for him, we were excited about all this opportunity could offer for our precious firstborn.

What came next, however, caught me completely off guard. It was suggested that we meet with the school's occupational therapist (OT) for an evaluation. Even though I saw zero need for it at the time, I also didn't see the harm in at least allowing the evaluation.

So I scheduled our appointment with Heidi Tringali.

As the evaluation concluded, she offered some suggestions for things we might work on to help our son, as well as a plan to see him regularly in her clinic until school started.

Until this point, our only exposure to OT was with our youngest son. But OT for him looked vastly different. At only two years old, he had already been diagnosed with a brain malformation, a severe seizure disorder, and cerebral palsy. He had a feeding tube, did not walk, did not talk, and was in and out of the hospital for a multitude of issues. In my eyes, OT was for children like him who had a host of diagnoses and very visible limitations.

I could not have been more misguided.

Over the next few years, both boys were enrolled in therapies. And while our youngest was able to make progress, various aspects of his life continue to limit his abilities.

What I was not prepared for was the impact OT, and Heidi specifically, had on not just our oldest son, but our entire family.

What was also new to me was that occupational therapy is not just for those experiencing major illness, disease, or disabilities. It literally feels like it's for everyone.

Everyone.

As our oldest began seeing Heidi regularly, in and out of school, my view of my role as a parent began to change. I was not going to be able to rely as heavily as I had assumed on my own childhood in trying to understand all that my son would need. Not to mention, I didn't grow up with brothers, so parenting boys was uncharted territory for me.

I needed a brand new lens.

The more I learned about how our world has changed for our kids, the more I began to grasp how vital it would be to develop this new lens through which to raise my children.

As our oldest son now makes his way through the last semester of his senior year in high school, I am amazed at how I am still tapping into all that I have learned (and continue to learn) from Heidi and her uncommon approach to OT.

Heidi's fun, compassionate, and whole-child/whole-family/whole-environment approach to helping our sweet children was life-changing for our family. Watching her transform our wiggly, frustrated, and sometimes struggling little boy into a more adjusted, calmer, and more confident child was not only fascinating, it was empowering. She doesn't keep secrets… she shares it all!

As a parent herself, she sees all of our kids as such beautiful gifts. Her goal is to help everyone connected to these children learn tools that provide a consistent voice. Those tools and that voice of consistency help establish a strong foundation on which our children get to build a solid framework that will serve them throughout their lives.

I'm not gonna lie, it ain't easy. It's sometimes an uphill battle with seemingly insurmountable obstacles. But there's that day. That moment in time when you use what you've learned or see your child apply tools that they have been taught, and you know it is changing their trajectory. It's those days that remind you it's all worth it.

The goal is not to change your child. The goal is to really see your child for who they are. To embrace how wonderfully they were stitched together and help them confidently take their place in the world.

That's what Heidi did and continues to do for our family. That's why her blend of deep compassion, practical tips, lighthearted humor, and endless patience has helped countless parents, educators, and other OTs make such a difference in the lives of families who never even knew they needed OT.

And now she has assembled her expansive knowledge, her decades of experience, and her incredible ability to "break it all down" into one invaluable resource.

Introduction

I am a *Pediatric Occupational Therapist.*

My path to becoming an Occupational Therapist began as a dream of being a special education teacher. I soon realized, however, that I was not designed to lead in the classroom setting. As I watched those teachers who balanced the needs of every child while still teaching a coherent lesson each day, I was in awe. Thank goodness for my college advisor, Dr. Jan Watkins. I am forever grateful to her for gently guiding me to Occupational Therapy.

A common question I am asked is, 'What is Occupational Therapy?' The simplest way to explain it is to think about what you do to *occupy* your time. Do you work, take care of yourself, take care of others, play a sport, go to school, or socialize? If you are unable to do any of these activities that typically *occupy* your time, an Occupational Therapist (OT) can help. OTs serve people of all ages, from premature babies learning to latch and nurse to the elderly working to maintain their independence. OTs can help with the smallest of tasks to some of the more involved everyday skills.

Our practice, Tringali Occupational Therapy Services (T.O.T.S), fills a unique niche in Occupational Therapy. We are a pediatric Occupational Therapy practice serving children with average to above-average intelligence who are underperforming relative to their potential.

We help families when their parenting journey goes astray or differs from what they expected. The children we serve are often struggling with the daily activities of learning, playing, and being family members. These struggles can lead to unexpected behaviors, emotions, and words. All of these *unexpecteds* can take a toll not only on the parents and child, but on the entire family unit.

The amazement I have experienced throughout my career is walking the journey with and seeing the transformation in these children and families. This professional path has given me a front-row seat to kids growing into the best versions of themselves, parents learning to see their children through a lens of success and possibility, and families coming together to celebrate the uniqueness that defines them.

I am a *mom.*

One of the greatest joys of my life is being a mom. I tend to be a meticulous planner. As part of my master plan, I intentionally waited until I was 35 to have children. By this age, I assumed I had reached a level of acceptable maturity, financial security, professional stability, education, and life experience to successfully parent a child. Those of you with children are likely having a good chuckle. Are we ever really ready?? I also believe God has a wonderful sense of humor and finds the whole planning aspect of parenthood a hoot!

Like many new parents, I viewed my young children through a lens of perfection. They were perfectly cute, smart, kind, and precious. On the park bench, I would catch myself playing the comparison game of whose child was mastering which skills first. And, through my lens of perfection, I believed my children were faring quite well. Fast forward over 20 years, and I can tell you without hesitation that my parenting journey was anything but perfect. And my lens of perfection has transformed into a lens of perspective. The struggles of family, marriage, parenting, and life are real and sometimes brutal. Trying to discern the important from the urgent and the necessary from the unnecessary can be downright daunting. In a world of content overload and mental/emotional/physical clutter, it can feel nearly impossible to stay focused on the task of raising children well.

Through these struggles, experiences, and God's grace-filled design, I have gained a perspective that now allows me to join other parents as they travel their own beautiful and sometimes treacherous journey. I view my successes, failures, and struggles as a mother with gratitude, as they allow me to provide some light in the darkness to families who are feeling a little lost.

I am a *believer.*

What that means is God is my why. My faith is the anchor of my work. Any amount of compassion or hope I offer is because of Him. Any wisdom or creativity I have to share comes from Him.

I grew up in a family of believers, but it wasn't until I had children that I truly understood what it meant to fully rely on God. As I was learning to rely on Him, I realized that I, too, am aspiring to be a readied child. As a child of God, I want to be ready for the calling He has placed on my life.

As a mom, I now fondly look back on one particularly long evening with our newborn. We were struggling through a sleepless night, and I remember praying something along the lines of, "God, if you get us through this, I promise to help every other struggling parent out there." Over 20 years later, God has more than held up His end of the deal.

This book is me holding up mine.

Start Here

You've most likely picked up this book because something's askew in your parenting world.

Your child continues to have trouble falling asleep despite trying every tip you can find.

Yet another note was sent home from your son's teacher because he disrupted class… again.

Your family has yet to have a dinner where your child remains seated for more than five minutes at a time.

It doesn't seem as though your child will ever make a friend.

You're exasperated. You're tired. You are out of ideas.

You might feel frustrated or like you just can't get it right. Or, maybe it feels like everything you try is unsuccessful.

You might have experienced situations where both you *and* your child walk away worn out and fed up.

This book is for you if you feel like you have exhausted all the tools in your *Parenting Toolbox* and nothing is working.

Maybe you feel like you have nothing left.

This book is for you if you are consumed with worry or maybe something is just nagging your parent heart.

Oh, that parent heart. The heart that came into existence when we were given the most incredible gift of nurturing and guiding our children in this world.

But the world wants to silence your parent heart and your natural instincts. Through emotional advertising, many companies aim to instill fear, guilt, scarcity, and comparison, prompting you to endlessly seek and continually doubt.[1] But *you* are the gatekeeper. It is *your* job to intentionally decide whose opinions, thoughts, and words get to enter your head, heart, and home. The world wants to convince you that you need more. More advice, more opinions, more things. That you are less than or possibly not good enough or knowledgeable enough to raise your own child.

> You are the gatekeeper. You decide whose opinions and words enter your head, heart, and home.

The child you've been given.

The child for whom you were hand-picked and perfectly designed.

Before you read another paragraph, I want to reassure you. You were flawlessly designed and masterfully selected to parent the child in front of you. You are *more than enough* for your child. You, by design, are perfect for your child.

The purpose of this book is not to tell you how to parent your child, but to introduce you to the concept of the **Readied Child**. A *Readied Child* is one who is equipped with the tools they need to perform to their fullest potential when faced with any demand or challenge. It

---

1   Indeed Editorial Team. "25 Types of Emotional Appeal Advertising (With Tips)." *Indeed Career Guide*, Indeed, 16 Dec. 2025. https://www.indeed.com/career-advice/career-development/emotional-appeal-advertising. Accessed 30 July 2025.

doesn't mean they are perfect or never without struggles. It means they have developed the tools and self-awareness they need to self-advocate and contribute to the world in a meaningful way with the gifts they have been given. This book is designed to help you develop a new lens through which to view your child and add new tools to your parenting toolbox.

We all have a parenting toolbox, whether we realize it or not. Your toolbox may already feel quite full of strategies from your upbringing, tips from the latest blogs and podcasts, and recommendations from the current top parenting experts.

I am not going to simply add more tools to an already stressed, and some might say, cluttered, toolbox. As you work your way through each chapter, together we will sort through your toolbox. Consider it a spring cleaning of sorts. We will set aside some of your less effective tools, and you may even choose to eliminate some outdated ones. But more importantly, I will equip you with new strategies.

This book has tools:

- that help your child when they can't remember simple things like what they need to bring home for homework.
- to improve their organization with things like following multi-step directions.
- to use when your child is too wiggly or struggles with body control or coordination.
- for social skill development when your child struggles in playgroups or playdates.
- for when your child seems socially disconnected or unavailable.
- for how to respond when your child is melting down or throwing a fit.

These are a few of the new strategies you will learn throughout this book. With these tools comes a new lens that will fill you with renewed confidence in your ability to guide your child from birth to launch.

A new lens of seeing your child through potential and readiness rather than behaviors and problems.

A more accurate lens that will allow you to see the beauty in all the uniqueness that defines your child, while giving you some new, and might I add, fun tips and techniques to meet your child's needs.

As you invest in utilizing this new lens, you begin to empower your child to head out into the world, ready to use all of their God-given talents to the fullest.

This book is different from most parenting books. I challenge you to read it with an openness that will silence the noise of the world and the voices saying you are not enough. An openness that will silence the voices that tell you your *child* is somehow broken or failing. A primary reason I do what I do every day is to help parents and children reconnect on a deeper level of understanding, respect, and empowerment. Allow this book to offer a new lens that will bring peace and make sense to your parent heart.

> Allow this book to offer a new lens that will bring peace and make sense to your parent heart.

The Misunderstood Child and an Equal Opportunity for Mediocracy

Typically, pediatric Occupational Therapists serve children who are performing below their age, grade, or developmental level. In public schools, we have extensive services for children performing *below grade level*. Those students receive support through an IEP (Individualized Education Plan), 504 (an academic accommodation plan), or a variety of other academic support services.[2] If a child is functioning *at grade level,* they will be placed in a general education classroom. If a child is performing *above their grade level,* they will be served through a Gifted and Talented program. However, there are no services for high-IQ students performing at grade level. When a child with a high IQ is performing below their potential but at grade level, there are no identified problems, thereby suggesting that, in America, we have equal opportunity for mediocrity. Unfortunately, there are no interventions available for this child, and he will move through the school system unsupported.

Any child underperforming relative to their potential is a frustrated and often misunderstood child. The child underperforming for their *potential* is as frustrated as the child underperforming for their *grade level.* Meeting the needs of children underperforming for their potential is where my passion lies. Every child should be given the opportunity to reach their full potential.

> Every child should be given the opportunity to reach their full potential.

While our OT practice typically serves children with healthy IQs, this book is written with a broader focus on every child's strengths and on establishing learning readiness regardless of intelligence or skill. Ironically, the tips, tools, and techniques related to learning readiness apply not only to almost every child but also to many adults, as well.

To Diagnose or Not Diagnose

There are times when labels and diagnoses are appropriate. Timing is essential, though, because it is difficult to remove those labels once they have been given. When children are younger (from preschool

---

2   "IEPs vs. 504 Plans." *National Center for Learning Disabilities,* 6 Jan. 2024, ncld.org/ieps-vs-504-plans/. Accessed 30 July 2025.

through early elementary), there is much we can do to help them develop the skills needed to overcome many of the challenges they face. During the toddler and early preschool years, it can be difficult to differentiate between deficits, delays, and normal development. There is, however, a time and place to explore various diagnoses to help families receive the support they need to properly care for their child. If your child is dealing with serious physical, mental, emotional, or psychological challenges, continue to seek and utilize the professional help that will best support your child's needs.[3]

Tips and Tricks for Getting the Most Out of This Book

As you read *The Readied Child*, your idea of parenting success will be challenged. For many parents I work with, it takes some time to embrace these new ideas and concepts. You will likely shift your parenting goals from ones focused on happiness and achievement to ones that include a better understanding of readiness. But we'll travel this road together. We will tackle parenting insecurities and discuss how to stabilize your parenting plan even in the midst of the unexpected.

Together, we will examine, sort through, reorganize, and enrich your Parenting Toolbox. We'll add easy-to-understand tips to address the questions parents most often ask when I'm working with their family in our clinic or during in-person presentations. We are on this journey together.

Some of the topics may not apply to your current family situation, and some may hit a little too close to home. But don't give up. Read through the entire book and then maybe read through it again with pen in hand. Highlight, make notes, and mark pages that are of significant

---

3   Bailey, Anne. "What Is a Psychoeducational and Giftedness Child Assessment and Who Is It For?" *Springboard Clinic*, 21 Aug. 2024, springboardclinic.com/what-is-a-psychoeducational-and-giftedness-child-assessment-and-who-is-it-for/. Accessed 30 July 2025.

importance to you. And keep the book as a reference for future use. My hope is that this book is torn, tattered, and beloved as you keep turning back to it while you learn to delight in the many dimensions of parenting your child.

Welcome to *The Readied Child*!

Author's Notes

The activities in this book should be performed only under adult supervision, with safety always in mind. The activities should be modified to meet each child's abilities.

The pronouns 'he' and 'she' used in this book are simply for consistency and ease of reading. Boys and girls benefit equally from this information and these strategies.

This book is in no way intended to replace the Occupational Therapy services your child is currently receiving or may need in the future.

CHAPTER 1
Kids These Days!

To better understand the premise of *The Readied Child* and what learning readiness means, we must first examine the history of childhood development. Over the past 40+ years, significant societal shifts have impacted how children learn and grow. In this chapter, as we dive into the details, you'll see how their everyday lives, particularly related to movement and physical activity, continue to be affected.

Each generation laments the changes of the generation that follows it. It's the idea that 'kids these days' don't really understand, they get away with things we never would have, and they do not respect authority the way we once did. Today's children are being shaped by more social influences than previous generations. The following sections can be somewhat heavy to read and a lot to take in, but I encourage you to pay close attention to the many ways we have inadvertently impeded our

> Today's children are being shaped by more social influences than previous generations.

children's movement and physical development. Yet, when you get through this book, you will find there is hope on the other side… for kids *these* days.

Back to Sleep

Between 1992 and 1994, the National Institute of Child Health and Human Development (NICHD) and the American Academy of Pediatrics (AAP) launched a public health initiative called ***Back to Sleep***. The purpose of the initiative was to reduce the number of Sudden Infant Death Syndrome (SIDS) and Sudden Unexpected Infant Death Syndrome (SUID)-related deaths among newborns.[4] We were encouraged to place our infants on their 'backs to sleep' as the safest sleep position. Prior to the Back to Sleep Initiative, it was estimated that approximately 4,000-5,000 children died each year of SIDS.[5] Because of the Back to Sleep initiative, infants were sleeping on their backs, the number of deaths was significantly reduced, and the campaign was considered successful.[6]

Although the initiative was successful, the recommendation to place babies on their tummies to play was overlooked. We became so focused on 'back to sleep,' we never really gave much thought to *tummy time*. As a result, we began leaving babies on their backs for

---

4   Centers for Disease Control and Prevention. "Trends in SUID Rates by Cause of Death, 1990–2022." *Data and Research: SIDS Deaths by Cause*, National Center for Chronic Disease Prevention and Health Promotion, U.S. Department of Health and Human Services, 17 Sept. 2024, www.cdc.gov/sudden-infant-death/data-research/data/sids-deaths-by-cause.html. Accessed 30 July 2025.

5   "Data and Statistics for SUID and SIDS." *Centers for Disease Control and Prevention*, National Center for Chronic Disease Prevention and Health Promotion, 17 Sept. 2024, www.cdc.gov/sudden-infant-death/data-research/data/index.html. Accessed 30 July 2025.

6   Moon, Rachel Y., et al. "Sleep-Related Infant Deaths: Updated 2022 Recommendations for Reducing Infant Deaths in the Sleep Environment." *Pediatrics*, vol. 150, no. 1, 2022, e2022057990. *PubMed, https://pubmed.ncbi.nlm.nih.gov/35726558/*. Accessed 23 Dec. 2024.

extended periods of time, even while they were awake, all in the name of safety.

As the campaign continued to have success, the toy industry jumped on board and further refined the already popular arched toy structure used to entertain children while they were placed in a supine (flat on their back) position. These toy structures were marketed as a 'safe' play space for infants lying on their backs with toys dangling (safely) above their heads. Infants began spending more and more time on their backs, not just during sleep, but throughout the day as well.

Back to Sleep created an estimated 40-60% decline in SIDS,[7] and with that came a 400-600% increase in positional head deformities. Because children were now spending increased time on their backs, many developed ***Positional Plagiocephaly*** (Flat Head Syndrome).[8] In response to this, the corrective helmet industry gained measurable traction with a new, custom-fit, cranial remolding orthosis (baby helmet). Once a child had developed flat head syndrome, it was difficult to deny the need for these baby helmets, which had to be worn by babies 23 hours every day.

Both the arched toy structures and baby helmets became commonly accepted tools for new parents.

Eventually, the Back to Sleep campaign evolved into the Safe to Sleep campaign as we began to understand there was more to SIDS and sleep-related deaths in infants than simple positioning.

---

7   Marshall, Judith M., and Farooq Shahzad. "Safe Sleep, Plagiocephaly, and Brachycephaly: Assessment, Risks, Treatment, and When to Refer." *Pediatric Annals*, vol. 49, no. 10, 1 Oct. 2020, pp. e440–e447, doi:10.3928/19382359-20200922-02. Accessed 30 July 2025.

8   "Deformational Plagiocephaly." *Johns Hopkins Medicine*, Johns Hopkins Medicine, www.hopkinsmedicine.org/health/conditions-and-diseases/deformational-plagiocephaly. Accessed 30 July 2025.

The revisions included recommendations for firm sleep surfaces, no bumpers, appropriate room temperature, reduced co-sleeping, and no stuffed animals in the sleep area.[9] Even though the focus of safer sleeping practices has evolved, the changes brought about by the Back to Sleep campaign continue to be observed in the homes of new families today, and some infants still spend extended time lying inactively on their backs while awake. The most notable effects of the Back to Sleep campaign on child development include decreased upper-extremity strength, reduced core and neck strength, and delayed crawling, rolling, and sitting. In older children, this can look like poor posture, limited endurance, and weak fine motor skills. If this were the only trend impacting childhood development, it would be significant, but unfortunately, there's more.

Five-Point Car Restraints

Between 1978 and 1985, every state in the country passed a law mandating that children be restrained in car seats while in a moving vehicle.[10] Just like Back to Sleep was intended to save lives by reducing the number of SIDS-related deaths, car seats were intended to keep children safe and alive while riding in cars. These laws have been highly successful, when implemented correctly, in saving children's lives in motor vehicle accidents.

By law, car seats are mandatory for children in cars.

In cars being the most crucial part of that sentence.

---

9   Eunice Kennedy Shriver National Institute of Child Health and Human Development. "Campaign History." *Safe to Sleep®*, U.S. Department of Health and Human Services, National Institutes of Health, safetosleep.nichd.nih.gov/campaign/history. Accessed 30 July 2025.

10   Pratt, Michelle. "The History of Car Seats." *Safe in the Seat Blog*, 19 Oct. 2024, www.safeintheseat.com/post/the-history-of-car-seats. Accessed 30 July 2025.

The purpose of a car seat is to safely secure a child into the seat of the car to prevent injury or death during a car accident, and I 100% stand behind this law. I am in no way promoting transporting any child unrestrained in a motor vehicle.

Using a different lens, let's take a look at this from the perspective of motor development.

"Motor development is the progressive acquisition of functional abilities of the child that reflect the maturation of the structures of the Central Nervous System that support them."[11]

Envision a child in a five-point harness car seat. There are straps over each shoulder, one at each hip, and one between the legs. Add in side-impact protection (blinders) and a rear-seat entertainment system, and we have essentially rendered our children immobile. Often their eyes are fixed on a screen in front of them, and the sensory input children received in past years from the natural movement in a car is restricted and essentially nonexistent. Because we have limited the types of physical input children used to receive during a simple car ride, today it is more important than ever to allow activities in their daily lives that mimic movements like rolling onto the floorboards, being tossed to the other side of the seat during a sharp turn, watching traffic signs and trees shoot by at 60 mph, or putting your arms on the seat in front of you bracing for a sudden stop.

Child car restraints may have had less negative impact if children only sat in them while seated in a moving vehicle, as the law requires. *But,* instead, a handle was added, essentially turning them into 'baby buckets.' These baby buckets fit securely in strollers, rest nicely in grocery carts, and are easily placed on countertops for feedings and ease of accountability.

---

11 García Pérez, M. A. "Psychomotor Development and Warning Signs." *Pediatrics Update Course*, edited by MGM, 2016, pp. 81–93.

To fully grasp the impact of car seats on childhood development, I like to share a story my mom frequently told. My parents drove a 1960 Chrysler 300F, and seatbelts were more decorative than necessary. The front seat did not have the large center console that many cars have today, so imagine a long bench seat in both the front and the back. My mom, who had an affinity for speed, also had a keen eye for police cars. She wasn't a big fan of speeding tickets, so when she saw a police officer, she would slam on the brakes to get as close to the speed limit as quickly as possible. In 1963, as she was driving my infant brother home from a doctor's appointment, she spotted a police car. True to form, she slammed on the brakes, and my brother swiftly rolled off the car seat onto the floor of the car. When I first heard this story, I visualized my brother in the back seat, in a five-point harness car seat, and couldn't understand why he would end up on the floor. It took me a few minutes to realize they didn't use infant car restraints back then. Not the kind we use for babies today, at least. In those days, babies were often simply placed on the front seat of the car next to the parents, much like we place our purse or bag next to us today. When my mom slammed on the brakes, my brother abruptly log-rolled to the floor.

Side note—he is fine and has no injuries from the event.

Many of my childhood memories include unrestrained car rides. Standing up in the back of the car or lying in the back window, watching things zoom by at 70-80 mph, with the occasional police sighting that would send us all rolling onto the floorboards.

During these car rides, when children were unrestrained, they engaged in movements that benefited their development. They were learning how to balance and stabilize their core muscles; their eyes were moving naturally in ways that developed depth perception and linear pre-reading skills; and their sense of where they were in space was enriched by bumping, rolling, and moving.

As I reflect on those childhood experiences as an adult, I have to laugh. I have wonderful memories of being tossed around the backseat and staring out the window at everything we drove past. As an Occupational Therapist, I appreciate the natural development that came from those unrestrained rides. However, as a law-abiding, common-sense-informed citizen, I've never heard of a less responsible way to transport children and loved ones.

I feel it is essential to reiterate that I am not advocating for children riding unrestrained, and I actually strongly support continuing to secure your children in car seats during all automobile travel. I am, however, encouraging you to leave the car seat in the car. Instead, when not in a car, consider carrying your baby and letting your toddlers walk and run.

As children transition from infants to toddlers, they move from extended time on their backs to extended time restrained in 'baby buckets,' thereby muting two vital components of the childhood experience: motor development and muscle strengthening. Not only are children missing out on opportunities to build these skills, but they are also being prohibited from these opportunities in the name of safety and convenience. Now, it is more important than ever to get them out to play on the floor and on their tummies. Work with them on head control, rolling over, crawling, and pulling up. Allow your children to walk, run, skip, hop, fall down, get up, and fall again. Provide opportunities for them to swing and bounce, turn upside down, and get a little dizzy. When my children were little, I often had to remind myself that infancy and the toddler years are simply

> Infancy and the toddler years are simply a brief training season for the marathon of life.

a brief training season for the marathon of life. Even though it may feel like we don't have time for these little extras, making small changes like this will improve your children's core strength, body awareness, and eye development, all of which are necessary for their long-term success.

Keep these strategies in mind as we explore another facet that has impacted our children in both their daily lives and their long-term health—the sedentary world of screen time.

Screen Time

Before the invention of television in the 1920s, screen time referred to the amount of time an actor spent on the screen.[12] However, over time, the term has evolved and now describes the amount of time a person spends in front of a screen—watching TV, playing video games, using a computer, tablet, phone, or other smart device, including time spent on social media.

As technology expanded, so did our ideas for incorporating screens into our everyday lives. We began to see the benefits of screen time in learning, play, and convenience. Soon, screen time and video games were touted as valuable and widely accessible tools that helped our children become smarter, faster. These tools were, and continue to be, viewed as effective for teaching social skills, emotional regulation, and self-care. Screens are also often viewed by some as the highest form of entertainment and/or quality childcare.[13] But the research is clear, and none of what we initially thought is true. It suggests that

---

12 Arora, Rijul. "The Evolution of Screen Time: A Historical Perspective." *Blog on Digital Wellness*, 12 Sept. 2025, rijularora.com/blog/the-evolution-of-screen-time-a-historical-perspective. Accessed 30 July 2025.

13 Child Trends. "5 Ways Screen Time Can Benefit Children and Families." *Child Trends*, 2018, www.childtrends.org/publications/5-ways-screen-time-can-benefit-children-and-families. Accessed 30 July 2025.

the effects of screens on the developing brain are overwhelmingly detrimental to development across all areas—intellectual, social, emotional, and physical.[14]

Screens have introduced an increasing level of inactivity we have never seen before. Because we now use screens in almost every aspect of life, our children have lost opportunities to grow in very natural, typical ways. This inactivity is quite literally destroying our children's childhood, causing delays in motor development, self-regulation, muscle strength, and social development. Things like climbing a tree and jumping rope have been replaced by electronic gaming systems. Instead of riding bikes and spending time with friends in real life, our kids are interacting with people remotely online.

As we gain a deeper understanding of childhood development, it becomes clear how crucial movement is to our children. From spending excessive time on their backs, in baby buckets, and in front of screens, our children are missing out on vital opportunities to build muscle, learn how to get on and fall off their bikes, get along with others, regulate their bodies by hanging upside down, and even tolerate something as simple as getting hot and sweaty.

> As we gain a deeper understanding of childhood development, it becomes clear how crucial movement is for our children.

In the same vein, the No Child Left Behind law was a well-intentioned program designed to ensure high-quality education for all children, regardless of zip code. However, the program failed, further immobilizing our preschool children with tasks such as reading and writing. Their bodies were not designed for this level of restricted

---

14 Karani, N. F., J. Sher, and M. Mophosho. "The Influence of Screen Time on Children's Language Development: A Scoping Review." *South African Journal of Communication Disorders*, vol. 69, 2022, pp. 0–7, doi:10.4102/sajcd. v69i1.825.

movement at such a tender age. Let's explore the residual impact of this now-repealed law.

No Child Left Behind (NCLB)

In 2002, the No Child Left Behind (NCLB) law was passed by the United States federal government.[15] The law focused on creating an achievement-based accountability system for all schools to improve the quality of education, especially in impoverished areas. The idea behind the law was commendable, but one particularly negative consequence arose from a section known as the Early Reading First (ERF) program.[16] Simply put, Early Reading First crammed kindergarten academics into preschools under the guise of "kindergarten readiness." Through this program, preschools received federal funding when they taught reading and writing to prepare children for the demands of kindergarten.

Childhood experts agree that most preschool-aged children are not ready for these demands. However, due to the Early Reading First initiative, preschools began incorporating academics into their curricula. Unfortunately, this change altered the dynamics of all preschools, and, under the expectations of Early Reading First, preschool teachers were expected to incorporate reading and writing into their daily lesson plans, all in the name of kindergarten readiness. The underlying message: to prepare a child for kindergarten, we must teach kindergarten skills earlier.

---

15 *Fact Sheet: No Child Left Behind Has Raised Expectations and Improved Results. The Bush Record: Fact Sheets*, The White House, 2006, georgewbush-whitehouse.archives.gov/infocus/bushrecord/factsheets/No-Child-Left-Behind. html. Accessed 30 July 2025.

16 U.S. Office of Management and Budget. "Early Reading First." *ExpectMore. gov: Program Assessment Summary*, U.S. Office of Management and Budget, 2006, obamawhitehouse.archives.gov/sites/default/files/omb/assets/omb/ expectmore/summary/10003322.2006.html. Accessed 30 July 2025.

Years ago, kindergarten was where children learned skills such as taking turns, sharing, standing in line, using materials safely and correctly, coloring, cutting, skipping, and developing self-regulation. As women began to join the workforce, preschools gained popularity. As the prevalence of preschools grew, these readiness skills were included in the standard preschool curriculum, and reading and writing became the norm in kindergarten and first grade.

Even if your child is not enrolled in a federally funded program, this change is impacting him/her. In today's world, we are constantly comparing our children in conversations with other parents at the playground, at birthday parties, through social media, and during sports practices. Parenting has become a competitive sport. Instead of focusing on what's developmentally appropriate or what "learning readiness" truly means, we are now gauging our child's readiness for kindergarten through the imperfect, false lens of the highest-performing child. We are encouraged to focus on how quickly our children master academic skills instead of on building a foundation of skills that allows them to perform to their fullest potential in any setting or circumstance. As the anxiety levels rise in parents, so does the enlistment of academic tutors to help prepare children for kindergarten. Because of this new academic expectation in preschool, our preschool teachers, who are experts in teaching classroom-readiness skills, are also teaching academics. Conversely, our kindergarten and first-grade teachers, who are experts in teaching reading and writing, are now having to teach skills such as standing in line, not touching one's friends, self-regulation, and managing and caring for classroom materials. Children are showing up to kindergarten with letter recognition and beginning reading skills, but are unable to hold a thought, wait without

> **Parenting has become a competitive sport.**

entertainment, or respond appropriately to a voice of authority, which can disrupt the rich educational environment of the classroom.

As we mentioned at the beginning of this chapter, these topics are heavy. Understanding how we arrived at this point is crucial to determining the most effective way to support your child. The same heaviness also applies to the next section, which covers topics of fear, the internet, and COVID-19. Once we have covered the details of how our children have been impacted, we can begin to learn and embrace the many ways we can help them flourish.

Fear, the internet, and COVID-19

Reading all this information might elicit feelings of concern, over-whelm, anxiety, or even fear. When you hear the word fear, what is the first thing that comes to mind? For me, it makes me think of the anxiety associated with what *might* happen. It brings about worry related to things in the future, how they may play out, and the various ways I could handle them. But it also robs me of the present moment.

With regard to parenting, fear not only drives decisions we make about our children, but prolonged fear, resulting in ongoing worry and anxiety, affects our well-being and the efficacy of our parenting. This can have lasting effects on the way our children grow and develop.

Reasonable fear protects us from danger, but excessive fear can have detrimental health effects. So, what pushes us over the edge from fear to excessive fear? One culprit in this generation is the excessive access to information. We have access to every imaginable type and amount of information. Just as with fear, a healthy amount of information is essential, but when we are over-informed, we can become mentally immobilized.

As previously presented in this chapter, the introduction of screen time has had an overwhelmingly negative impact on young children.

But the damage isn't limited to just childhood. Ironically, a quick Google search revealed that, "With the internet at our fingertips with smartphones, we are exposed to an unprecedented amount of data far beyond our ability to process. The result is an inability to evaluate information and make decisions."[17]

Now, imagine that information related to parenting.

When we are overinformed—unable to distinguish between what is truly valuable and what is simply additional information—the soil is prepped and ready for fear and anxiety to take root. Instead of seeking the counsel of trusted members of prior generations, passing down wisdom from tested and proven parenting methods, and being intentional about how (and from whom) we gather parenting information, we search and scroll looking for a quick fix to whatever ailment or issue with which we are currently dealing. Add to that our reduced attention span[18] (thank you, three-second reels), and we cannot stick to one thing long enough to see if it actually works. Fearing that we have not yet found the correct information, we move on to the next thing, and the process repeats. And it repeats and repeats and repeats.

This rapid-fire-answer-seeking approach we use has immobilized us, leading us to think we are no longer capable of making simple, basic decisions for our children. We consult a multitude of relatively unknown online sources, trying to find reassurance that we are making the right call when it comes to our kids. Not only is this fear-producing, but it's exhausting.

---

17 Rensselaer Polytechnic Institute. "Information Overload Is a Personal and Societal Danger." *RPI News*, 13 Mar. 2024, https://news.rpi.edu/2024/03/13/information-overload-personal-and-societal-danger. Accessed 30 July 2025.

18 The Varsity. "Scroll, Swipe, Repeat: How Social Media Is Rewiring Our Attention Span." *The Varsity*, 15 Sept. 2024, thevarsity.ca/2024/09/15/scroll-swipe-repeat-how-social-media-is-rewiring-our-attention-span/. Accessed 30 July 2025.

As if all of this were not enough to send us over the edge, let's add a global pandemic to the mix. One of the most fear-influenced times in recent history was the COVID-19 pandemic of 2020.[19] This created, in most humans, a multitude of fears. A fear of dying from the virus, of spreading the virus, of losing our jobs, of not being able to protect our loved ones, and of the unknown. We expanded our vocabulary to include terms such as masking, social distancing, working remotely, quarantining, and sanitizing. And while we adopted all of these new practices, the lifestyle changes we made to accommodate COVID-19 only increased the prevalence of childhood developmental delays in social skills, sustained attention, risk-taking, and independent problem-solving.[20]

Recall your child's age during the pandemic. Now, think about what skills they would have typically been learning and mastering during that stage. For children at any age, the opportunity to develop social, emotional, physical, and cognitive skills during the pandemic was essentially nonexistent. Not to mention the isolation, which did not provide a healthy environment for anyone. During such a trying and fear-soaked time in our world's history, it's essential to examine what children may have missed that was crucial to their development. Instead of consulting the internet and filling our parent hearts with all the fear of what could be, let's begin to look at our kids through a new lens of what skills they need and how we can help them learn those skills.

---

19 Mertens, G., et al. "Managing Fear During Pandemics: Risks and Opportunities." *BMJ Global Health*, vol. 8, no. 5, 2023, https://pmc.ncbi.nlm. nih.gov/articles/PMC10293863/. *PubMed Central*, PMC10293863. Accessed 30 July 2025.

20 *The Youngest Pandemic Children Are Now in School, and Struggling. The New York Times*, 1 July 2024, www.nytimes.com/interactive/2024/07/01/upshot/ pandemic-children-school-performance.html. Accessed 30 July 2025.

You made it through! This is a brutally difficult but necessary chapter to read, as it sets the stage for a better understanding of why children are struggling these days. In the following nine chapters, we will explore the various systems in the body that support the Readied Child. You'll read about inspiring real-world examples, easy-to-implement tools, and memorable information to help your children overcome setbacks and obstacles. Our goal is to help your child develop skills for a lifetime of learning readiness.

CHAPTER 2
Learning Readiness

"You also must be ready, because the Son of Man will come at an hour when you do not expect him."
(Luke 12:40)

Historically, the phrases 'ready for school' and 'ready to learn' have been used interchangeably. They both implied that when you arrived at your classroom, you were prepared for the day's demands. However, as we learned in the last chapter, numerous social and environmental influences have wreaked havoc on childhood development, and consequently, the terms 'learning readiness' and 'school readiness' no longer mean the same thing.

Being ready for school means that a child has gotten dressed, combed their hair, packed their backpack, and remembered to grab their lunch box. We can confidently say that they are ready for the school day, but are they ready for the demands of learning?

There are three characteristics that comprise being ready to learn.

They are being:

cognitively organized,

physically calm,

and ***socially connected***.

Many teachers have shared with me that they estimate approximately 30%-40% of the kids in their classroom are *not* ready to learn, as defined by being organized, calm, and connected. Let's take a closer look at this rising concern.

Cognitive organization refers to how the brain accepts, stores, and retrieves information. If your brain is organized, you can take in new information, store it efficiently, and retrieve it upon demand. Picture those children who play with purpose or can tell a story with a well-defined beginning, middle, and end. Or how about the ones who are articulate speakers, or the ones who can retrieve with ease information that they learned earlier? Those children have an organized brain.

So who are the kids with disorganized brains? Those kids are working overtime to meet the world's demands.

The sweetest five-year-old boy comes to see me at the clinic. When he arrives, he is so excited and tells me how much he loves all the activities! His eyes widen, and he looks around, trying to figure out where to start first. I gather him and his attention, reminding him that he can play with anything in the clinic, as long as he asks first. He enthusiastically agrees… and off he goes! He grabs the rope for a quick swing in only one direction before he jumps off and heads to the ladder. But before he can climb more than two rungs, he is back down and headed for the crash pad. He spends nearly a full three seconds jumping before he heads for one quick jump on the Bosu ball on the way to the trampoline. The trampoline jumping lasts for about 1.5 jumps before he notices the balloon. And this is a typical *start* to his OT session.

As his mom looks on in horror at his wild and purposeless play, I give her a gentle smile to remind her this is why they're here.

Another marker for cognitive disorganization is garbled speech. At one of the schools where we see a handful of kids, there is a quiet and very smart four-year-old boy. We travel down a very long hallway to the OT room, and the entire time, with his face pointed toward the floor, he mumbles. He is sharing all kinds of things with me that he wants me to know, but I strain to make out most of his words. Once in the OT room, he spins…and spins. And when we stop, he shares more about his family and their new pet with me. This time, he looks me in the eye, and I can understand every word. The spinning is not magic, but its effects of helping to organize his brain are absolutely fascinating. Purposeful, meaningful movement like this is one of the keys to readiness.

What about our ability to recall information that we have previously learned? While we all occasionally have trouble remembering things, another distinctive characteristic of a disorganized brain is difficulty retrieving previously learned information. I recently conducted an evaluation with a six-year-old boy. As I asked him various questions to see what he could recall, we started with his birthday. He told me his birthday was Thursday… which it wasn't. But he knew he was six. He said his dad's name was Daddy, but he couldn't recall his given name. He reported he had no siblings, and then told me a story about his brother. And he didn't know the name of the street he lives on, even though his mom said he knows his full address and talks about it all the time.

The second component of learning readiness is being physically calm. Many people think that being physically calm is the opposite of being excitable, but it actually lies between excitability and lethargy. Physical calm means that my body's need for or avoidance of movement isn't interfering with my ability to complete age-appropriate tasks. It means it isn't a distraction or obstacle to my ability to participate in life successfully.

So what does excitability and lethargy look like? Think of excitability as Tigger from Winnie the Pooh. It's the child who is constantly repositioning in their chair, the one who bolts out the door at recess, running and crashing through the playground, and the one who is seen trying to lift the heaviest items in the room. By contrast, consider Eeyore from Winnie the Pooh as an example of physical lethargy, which is associated with low arousal. They are the children who often appear to have low muscle tone, are frequently slumped over, exhibit little to no emotional response, and don't see the value in high-energy activities. These kids often do not want to move, avoid movement, or even feel fearful of movement. Both physical excitability and physical lethargy are obstacles to learning readiness.

The final trait, and the icing on the cake of learning readiness, is social connection. Being socially connected means you feel connected enough to others that what they say matters. At our core, humans crave, need, and are built for human relationships. In our culture today, we have normalized terms like introvert, autism, or 'too peopley' to describe, and sometimes justify, our disconnection. We then turn to things like screens to help fill our need for connection. However, screens cannot replace the natural deep pressure that our bodies previously experienced through activities like shaking hands, playing, and giving hugs. When given adequate deep pressure, our social connections improve, ultimately enhancing our readiness to learn.

In Chapter 1, we explored *why* our kids are struggling with learning readiness. In this chapter, we began by seeking to understand *what* readiness entails and by breaking down the three characteristics of the Readied Child. We dipped our toes into *how* to help our children ready their bodies when they are struggling (more details on this in upcoming chapters), and we will explore *where* all of this lives in Chapter 3.

But ***when*** does this actually happen?

Every day is filled with sequences of ***Ready–Demand–Response***. On any given day, we wake up and get *ready*. What we are preparing for is the *demand* placed on us that day. How well we *respond* to that demand, or those demands, determines our performance or the success of our day. When I'm ready (organized, calm, and connected), I can tolerate the demands (learning, recalling, working) and respond or perform at my fullest potential. If I show up to any demand disorganized, excitable, and disconnected, all bets are off. My performance or response will be unpredictable or subpar. When I show up unprepared, I may appear less intelligent or apathetic. A lack of learning readiness is fertile ground for a misunderstood child.

When discussing learning readiness in this book, we examine it through the lens of a child's achievement and performance; however, the concepts of being organized, calm, and connected apply to all humans. We all strive for a sense of *readiness and preparedness*.

> We all strive for a sense of readiness and preparedness.

Have you noticed that when you start your day feeling organized, calm, and connected, your level of achievement increases? You feel more equipped to fulfill your responsibilities on those days. You may also notice that on those days, parenting is easier.

But what about those days when you are not organized? Or when you are feeling less than calm? Or when you are not as socially connected? When your brain feels disorganized, your body is either excitable or lethargic, and you feel socially disconnected from others, you will feel anything but ready to tackle the world. It's on those days that your effectiveness and productivity suffer, which can often lead to feelings of inadequacy and incompetence.

The same is true for our kids.

When children are not ready to learn, meaning they are disorganized, excitable, and/or disconnected, they too will struggle to achieve success or develop a sense of accomplishment. Instead of success, one or more of the following is likely to occur:

- They will experience challenges in following multi-step directions.

- They will be reprimanded for excessive movement or activity.

- They will struggle with maintaining eye contact.

- Their responses to requests will be outside the norm.

- They may seem unaffected by consequences.

The simple truth is, they were not *ready* for the *demand* placed upon them. When this happens, they can feel overwhelmed and frustrated. They can struggle to pull it all together, and therefore, their *response* falls well below their potential.

Readiness, or the lack thereof, can manifest differently at different ages.

We may all ready ourselves differently or need different things to get ready, but the goal is always the same: *to optimally respond to our daily demands.* Before we explore the various tools available to prepare ourselves, let's examine a couple of examples of children I see in our clinic. For the purposes of the book, we will refer to them as Mac and Sam.

Meet Mac

Mac is four years old. Mac shows up to preschool like a tornado. Each day, he drops his bookbag at the door and his coat a few steps later. He runs to the play area and trips over a chair on the way. When he gets there, he snatches a toy from sweet little Sadie. As she begins to cry, he runs to his best little friend, Charlie, and accidentally falls on top of him while bumping his head on the shelf.

It is March, and by this time in the school year, routines have been learned, and classroom rules should be easy to follow. But not for Mac. He continues to struggle with every aspect of being ready to learn, and as a result, his classroom performance is much lower than his true ability.

Hold onto the description of Mac, and let's meet Sam.

Meet Sam

Sam is fourteen. Sam is very bright and consistently earns A's and B's in all his classes. Based on his perceived intellect, everyone believes he should easily be a straight-A student. However, Sam has trouble submitting his completed assignments, and when he does, they are often wrinkled and torn from being shoved to the bottom of his bookbag. In addition to being challenged by completing his work, Sam struggles to remember essential tools for classroom success—his pencil, a notebook, and sometimes even a textbook. He is often allowed to retrieve the items from his locker, but when he opens it, he becomes overwhelmed by the chaos inside and ends up returning to class without the items… again.

Sam likes to stand during class when the rest of the students are sitting. He also likes to chew gum. If allowed, he would chew gum every waking hour, but since this is not an option, he regularly bites his nails or chews on his pencils.

During class projects, Sam is described as a student who struggles to keep up with his supplies. He frequently loses his calculator, has half-finished assignments, or misses key components on the rubric outlining what is expected of him.

Unfortunately, Sam is beginning to doubt his intelligence. He doesn't enjoy school even though he loves to learn. He is beginning to get frustrated about being called out and called down in the classroom, and he has started withdrawing from his friends.

Mac and Sam are both struggling with *readiness*. Neither is ready for the demands of school. Mac risks being identified as poorly behaved, while Sam risks being identified as apathetic. Both are very likely *misunderstood students*.

OT Tip

Readiness challenges can look like other, more significant issues: bad behavior, Attention Deficit Hyperactivity Disorder (ADHD), Learning Disabilities, Oppositional Defiance Disorder (ODD), or Autism Spectrum Disorder (ASD).

A disorganized brain may present as a learning disability.

An active body may be misunderstood as ADHD.

A socially disconnected child may seem autistic.

It is essential to first address any readiness issues before considering a diagnosis.

It is beneficial to work with the appropriate professionals to gain a deeper understanding of your child's specific challenges.

Mac and Sam represent a growing number of our children who, through no fault of their own, are functioning below their true potential. Some could argue that we are not even aware of their full potential until they have had a chance to experience the demands of the world in a state of readiness. Whether we are preparing our children for the challenges of school, the demands of the athletic field, or defending their beliefs, it is our responsibility as parents to ensure they are ready. We will explore tools and techniques throughout this book that will help you not only assess your child's struggles but also provide practical ways to help them build skills that will serve them for a lifetime.

It is vital that we, as parents, begin to view our children, not through a lens set by the world, but through a lens of readiness. Readiness is not only the foundation on which everything else builds, but also the foundation that allows our children to launch successfully into adulthood. A healthy launch doesn't magically occur when a child turns 18; it is the culmination of all the small things we do each day. These small, yet intentional things can be categorized into three subsections—Assess, Advocate, and Launch. Let's take a closer look at each of them.

Accurate Self-Assessment

Readiness is foundational for developing the skill of *accurate self-assessment*. A child who can accurately self-assess can easily identify and speak about their strengths with the same level of confidence as they speak about their areas for growth.

> Readiness is foundational for developing the skill of accurate self-assessment.

It is never too early to instill the ability to accurately self-assess. Children as young as four can begin developing this skill. A child doesn't learn to accurately self-assess by being told their strengths and areas for growth. They learn it most effectively by seeing us master and model it.

Let's practice.

Say aloud your parenting strengths using the same level of confidence as you describe your areas for growth.

Now tell them to another person. Have that person give you feedback as to whether you stated both with the *same level of confidence*.

How did you do?

If you are like me, you found this exercise challenging. After working on it for what has felt like years, I can now tell you my strengths and weaknesses as a pediatric OT, with the same level of confidence.

I'm really good at working with children and speaking to families.

I continue to struggle with keeping up with my documentation and dealing with insurance companies.

Confidently discussing our own strengths and weaknesses is typically not easy. Through the years, I have noticed some interesting trends with males and females. Girls tend to feel more attached to their shortcomings, while boys often feel more confident in their strengths. For everyone, the goal is to speak about both with the same level of confidence.

When we, as parents, learn to accurately self-assess, we are then able to model it for our children. As we become more comfortable, it becomes less about practicing this technique and more about the lens through which we view ourselves. When children, as well as adults, have an accurate view of themselves in relation to their strengths and weaknesses, they are well-equipped to leverage their strengths to positively impact the world and to seek support in areas that are more challenging for them.

> When we, as parents, learn to accurately self-assess, we are then able to model it for our children.

Independent and Accurate Self Advocacy

Once accurate self-assessment is established, kids can then *independently and accurately self-advocate* in their early teens. By this point, they have developed the ability to easily identify areas where they excel and those where they need help. This knowledge allows them to leverage their strengths and seek support for their deficits. Being able to identify what they can offer and advocate for what they need sets them up to engage in richer learning experiences and make more impactful contributions to society.

Successful Launch

Independent and accurate self-advocacy is the foundation for a *successful launch* into adulthood. Because they know what they have to contribute and how to ask for what they need, they are able to enter the world with a more meaningful sense of purpose. The sequence of accurate self-assessment, independent self-advocacy, and successful launch sets the groundwork for a rich and fulfilling life.

It is essential to acknowledge that success should not be confused with perfection. Being ready does not mean being perfect. It doesn't mean never making a mistake or falling short. It means being prepared for things within our control when demands are placed upon us.

> Being ready does not mean being perfect.

I recently talked with a dad whose daughter I started working with when she was four years old. She was a month into her freshman year of college, and she called to tell him about an experience she had on the first day of classes. He braced himself for the fallout that he had seen in the past from situations just like this, but instead, he could only hear confidence in her voice. As she told her dad how she handled it all, she even giggled a little about the craziness of the whole situation. This is an example of a successful launch.

There will still be plenty of uncontrollables in our children's lives, but giving them the tools to prepare their brains, bodies, and social availability leaves room for all the good things life has to offer. It leaves room for our children to achieve their full potential and fulfill their purpose here on earth. And isn't that all we really want for our kids?

CHAPTER 3

The Sensory System – Home of Learning Readiness

"For we are God's handiwork, created in Christ Jesus to do good works, which God prepared in advance for us to do."
(Ephesians 2:10)

The sensory system is where learning readiness lives. It is one of the most intriguing and sometimes confusing systems in the body. Let's take a look at some simple facts about this intricate system.

Everyone has one.

We learn through our sensory system.

The sensory system is foundational for learning readiness.

It is foundational for self and emotional regulation.

When it doesn't work properly, it can wreak havoc on childhood development.

This system fluctuates day-to-day.

Factors such as sleep, illness, environment, and allergies can impact the function of our sensory system.

Let's start with some labels and terms to clarify the complexity of this system. Sensory Processing Disorder (SPD), sensory dysregulation, and Sensory Integration Disorder (SID) are labels associated with the sensory system. Terms such as seeker, avoider, high arousal, low arousal, hypersensitive, hypo-sensitive, and modulation are also linked to discussions about the sensory system. While many people have heard of some of these terms, most people still can't accurately or concisely explain sensory processing challenges. They often describe the sensory system by using examples of its impact on them, their family, or their friends. The following examples illustrate children who have varying degrees of sensory differences.

A child who must have all the tags removed from his shirts.

A child who cannot bear to eat foods with different textures.

A child who cannot tolerate swinging or spinning and gets frequent motion sickness.

A child who finds it unbearable to hear the sound of flushing toilets.

Children who have difficulty with potty training.

Children who have trouble deciphering whether they're hot or cold

With the vast array of terms and labels and the few examples we shared, it's easy to see how the nuances of the sensory system can be difficult to understand.

Jean Ayres began documenting and researching sensory differences in the 1960s, and it has since been studied extensively. However, even with all the analysis of data and increasing prevalence of disorders related to the sensory system, SPD and SID are still not recognized by the medical community as diagnoses covered by health insurance. Instead, sensory issues tend to primarily be linked to diagnoses like Autism and Attention Deficit Hyperactivity Disorder (ADHD). And while many of these sensory examples are related to these two well-known diagnoses, many children who exhibit sensory processing differences do not fit the criteria for Autism or ADHD.

The critical thing to remember is that the sensory system is where learning readiness lives. To further understand this system and its components, we will use a hand as a visual.

The Sensory System

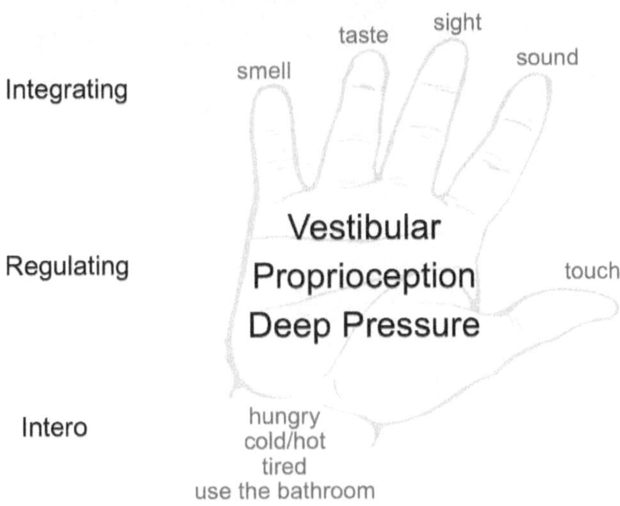

Some of us are familiar with the five senses we learned in kindergarten, while others have a deeper understanding of how the sensory system works within the body. For ease of understanding, in *The Readied Child*, we will discuss the relationship between the sensory system and *learning readiness*.

Should you wish to dive deeper into all things sensory, two of my favorite books are *Sensory Integration and the Child* by A. Jean Ayres, Ph.D., and *Understanding Your Child's Sensory Signals* by Angie Voss, MS, OTR/L.

The following breaks down and explains this system's three distinct parts: Sensory Integration, Sensory Regulation, and Interoception.

Sensory Integration – Integrating Senses

Sensory integration encompasses the five senses we learn about in kindergarten: **taste (oral), touch (tactile), sight (visual), smell (olfactory), and sound (auditory)**. These senses take in or *integrate* information from the world. We *learn* through these senses: seeing, hearing, touching, tasting, and smelling. These integrating senses can be considered our *learning senses*. Picture a child running barefoot along the sidewalk and then hopping onto the grass. They don't realize it, but their learning senses are teaching them what different surfaces feel like on their skin.

When a child learns through multiple senses simultaneously, it is called *multisensory learning*. Imagine looking at pictures of the ocean in a book while listening to a story about the sea, and then being allowed to touch and feel water and sand. This is a multisensory experience and is considered one of the most effective learning styles for children.[21] In fact, this is true for adults and children alike. We gain a deeper understanding and experience greater satisfaction when we learn by seeing *and* doing or smelling *and* tasting.

At any given time, these integrating senses can be *hypersensitive* (meaning overly sensitive) or *hypo-sensitive* (meaning under-sensitive). They can also be hypersensitive in the morning, then hyposensitive in the afternoon. Depending on the environment, one could actually fluctuate between hyper and hypo more rapidly. Some children can even show signs of hyper- and hyposensitivity at the same time.

---

21 Schukraft, Shari. "Multi-Sensory Learning: Types of Instruction and Materials." *IMSE Journal*, 20 Aug. 2020, journal.imse.com/multi-sensory-learning-types-of-instruction-and-materials/. Accessed 30 July 2025.

Let's use the auditory system, for example. If my auditory system is hypersensitive, sounds are too loud for me to tolerate. You might see a child covering their ears when exposed to loud sounds, or crying easily or intensely in response to an unexpected loud noise. On the other hand, auditory hypo-sensitivity means I prefer and seek loud sounds. I love loud noises, music, and TV, and I talk loudly. If there's no noise, I will make some of my own! My motto is: the louder, the better! These kids, and adults as well, might feel right at home in a rock band or working on a construction crew with a jackhammer! Then there's the child who covers their ears because someone else is too loud, while simultaneously making loud noises of their own. This child is experiencing both hyper and hyposensitivity at the same time. Imagine how that must feel!

Auditory sensitivity means that I register sound differently from other people. To process auditory information optimally, we want to fall somewhere in the middle, within the typical range of tolerance, rather than at the extremes of hyper- or hyposensitivity. And while this is simply a function of this child's sensory system, it is easy to see how an adult could view this as a behavioral issue and respond with behavior modification strategies. We'll discuss behavior modification later, but one clear indication that it's not a behavioral issue is when the punishment or reward doesn't work. If a punishment or reward doesn't produce the expected outcome, take a step back and ask yourself if this behavior might be related to the child's sensory system. You will most likely answer yes, it is a sensory regulation challenge.

A well-functioning sensory integration system is defined by the ability of the child's learning senses (the five senses) to take in information in a predictable manner, allowing the child to process, use, and store it for later use. But no one's sensory integrating system functions perfectly. For example, I don't wear wool or eat slippery food. As an adult, I manage this by wearing cotton clothes and avoiding oysters and "wet" scrambled eggs. However, our children do not always have an awareness of their sensory needs, the ability to express what they need, or the ability to control their sensory input. We all have sensory strengths and struggles, and throughout this book, we will explore ways to help your child incorporate tools and provide valuable input to their bodies to keep this system working optimally.

Sensory Regulation – Regulating Senses

Regulating senses are those that allow our brains to receive and respond to information from our integrating senses.

Learning occurs when new information is received through the integrating senses, and regulation is our body's *readiness* to receive and utilize it. This brings clarity and understanding to *where* learning readiness resides.

> Learning readiness dwells in our sensory system.

Learning readiness dwells in our sensory system.

Our regulating senses were designed to prepare, or regulate, our bodies to receive and process incoming sensory information. The three senses that comprise the regulating senses are our **vestibular**, **proprioceptive**, and **deep pressure** systems. We will explore each of these senses in great detail in upcoming chapters, but for now, we will examine their role in preparing our bodies to receive incoming information.

The first of the regulating senses is the *vestibular system*. This sense is responsible for balance, giving you awareness of the position of your head in space, and for cognitive organization. It is also responsible for symptoms like vertigo and motion sickness. The kids I mentioned earlier who simply could not tolerate swinging and spinning? That's their vestibular system saying, "No, no, it's too much, please stop!"

The second sense is the *proprioceptive system*, which tells you where your body is in relation to its surroundings. This is the system that is responsible for your sense of calm. Remember when I described the child who can't sit still in class? That child's proprioceptive system is saying, "We need more serotonin to keep this body still and stay calm enough to learn the lesson!"

And finally, the *deep pressure system*. This sense reads input through your skin and muscles, like hugs and squishes, and is responsible for giving you a sense of social connection. We become aware of this system when we see a child hold on too tightly or for too long when hugging their friends. Their deep pressure system is enjoying the small dose of dopamine, which allows them to feel connected to others.

The deep pressure sense is closely linked to the light touch/tactile system, which is part of the integrating senses. It can be confusing to keep them separate, but the easiest way to remember them is that the integrating (learning) light-touch system is for tags and tickles, and the regulating (readying) deep-pressure system is for hugs and squishes.

In the next three chapters, we will explore the regulating senses and the powerful role movement and sensory input play in learning readiness.

Interoception – Internal Senses

In the image of the hand from the first page of this chapter, the final group of senses is our ***interoceptive senses***. These senses are made up of the sensory receptors that line our internal organs.[22] These receptors tell us if we're tired, hungry or thirsty, hot or cold, and whether or not we have to use the bathroom. For children who have hypo-sensitivity in the sensory receptors around their bladder, they may not feel any of the first alerts of their body telling them it's time to go to the bathroom until their little bladder is at max capacity. When those receptors finally sense it, they send an urgent signal to the brain, and now these children are frantically begging you to pull the car over, or they are running from the middle of the store to the bathroom. Sometimes these alerts arrive so late that they may have an accident because they couldn't hold it a second longer. Without understanding how these receptors work or how they are connected to our sensory system, it's easy to blame the child for being lazy or not paying attention.

The opposite of this scenario would be hypersensitivity throughout the bladder's sensory receptors, in which case even the smallest amount of urine entering the bladder produces a sense of urgency, and they are constantly asking to use the bathroom. This scenario can be just as challenging to recognize when distinguishing between sensory dysregulation and behavior.

Children with interoception differences are often misunderstood as being picky, stubborn, odd, or difficult. When we help our children achieve a state of learning readiness, many of these interoception challenges resolve. Isn't that cool? It's just another reason I stand by the belief that our sensory system is one of the most intriguing systems in the human body.

> Children with interoception differences are often misunderstood as being picky, stubborn, odd, or difficult.

---

22 Pediatric Rehabilitation Services, Alberta Health Services. "Sensory Processing in Children." *MyHealth Alberta*, current as of 10 Mar. 2025, myhealth.alberta. ca/health/pages/4-sensory-processing-in-children.aspx. Accessed 30 July 2025.

Habituation

A healthy sensory system can ***habituate***, meaning our body can get used to something. By definition, it is the diminishing of a physiological or emotional response to a frequently repeated stimulus.[23] The following is an example of habituation.

You walk into a new place for the first time.

Your integrating senses get busy "reading the room."

Your visual sense takes in all the new sights.

Your tactile sense notices the humidity in the atmosphere and might even explore the texture of the walls, floors, and seats.

Your auditory sense notices the sounds of the HVAC system, planes flying overhead, or the squeaking of the floor as you walk across.

Your olfactory sense notices the smell of the diffuser in the space or might pick up the scent of what was cooked last night for dinner.

Using this example, when our sensory system settles in and comes off high alert, instead of focusing on all these details, it can focus on receiving only relevant and essential information—this is habituation. The relevant and essential information may be learning, working, talking, or listening. Through habituation, we are no longer distracted by the background things we noticed when we first entered the space, and we are able to be productive, efficient, and focused.

Without habituation, our sensory system stays on high alert and continues to process all competing inputs all day long. It can be truly exhausting! Take a moment and try to put yourself in the shoes of

---

23   Study.com. "Habituation: Overview & Examples." *Study.com*, 2023, study.com/academy/lesson/habituation-overview-examples-psychology.html. Accessed 30 July 2025.

a child who is trying to listen to a teacher's voice but is hearing the teacher with the same level of volume and intensity as they hear the air conditioner turning on and off, someone crumpling a piece of paper across the room, and the sound of another child whispering to a friend. Can you feel the overwhelm?

> They leave school more exhausted, more irritable, and often feeling more defeated than the child who can easily habituate.

They are working so much harder to learn and listen than the child who habituates easily. And that hard work comes at a cost. They come home from school more exhausted, more irritable, and often feeling more defeated than the child who can easily habituate.

Their day has been far more sensory-intense than that of their regulated peers.

The consequences of an inability to habituate affect not only how the child feels but also their academic performance and, often, their behavior. They are trying their best to hold it all together, but without the proper tools, this child often is misunderstood. When we help our children become regulated through vestibular, proprioceptive, and deep pressure activities, their ability to habituate improves. And another reason I find the sensory system so intriguing.

Sensory Profile

A *sensory profile* is a comprehensive, documented summary of a person's sensory status in all the areas we just covered. There are various standardized sensory profiles that can help one better understand one's sensory system. If everyone completed a sensory profile, the results would differ. And because these profiles are subjective, it is recommended that the sensory profile be completed as one portion of a more comprehensive assessment.

As mentioned earlier, my sensory profile would indicate I avoid eating slippery foods and dislike wearing wool. I also get car sick and struggle with balance. My vestibular, tactile, and taste systems are all hypersensitive. As an adult, I have developed strategies to overcome the challenges associated with my sensory profile. I wear cotton clothes, I never make or eat oysters or wet scrambled eggs, I always drive when traveling, and I quickly find a way to steady myself when walking on uneven surfaces. I have developed accommodations that are built into my daily life and very naturally allow me to function to my fullest potential despite my sensory differences.

Unfortunately, children aren't always able to identify and utilize accommodations for their sensory challenges. If a sensory-sensitive child walked into a classroom, turned off the lights because they were too bright, told everyone to be quiet, and told a couple of children they smelled bad, the outcome would not be favorable for that child. They would most likely get in trouble, be labeled poorly behaved, or be told they are difficult and rude. This situation leaves a child open to being misunderstood and inaccurately labeled, not to mention frustrated and sad.

It is *vital* that we understand the link between the sensory system and learning readiness. The sensory system is the key to knowing how to help our children achieve it.

The following three chapters are chock-full of specific examples, explanations, and strategies related to the vestibular, proprioceptive, and deep pressure sensory systems. The upcoming chapters pull it all together. Let's dive in!

OT Tip

With all the nuances we've covered regarding the sensory system and the varying sensory profiles, it becomes easier to understand the medical community's hesitancy to embrace Sensory Processing Disorder as a recognized diagnosis.

When we relate sensory differences to learning readiness, it is not as important to label them as it is to understand them. And for the sake of better understanding children and valuing the importance of learning readiness, it is vital that we understand the sensory system and how it influences our capacity to perform to our fullest potential.

On the contrary, it becomes important to have a label or diagnosis when the sensory system is so compromised that it severely impacts a child's life. An example of this is a child who is unable to leave their home because their sensory tolerances are too impaired. Or a child who can't enjoy a playground because the sensory experiences are too overwhelming. When a child is unable to participate in life, or their sensory needs become a significant burden on the family unit, it may be time to seek professional help. Without a label or diagnosis, a child who needs professional intervention but is unable to afford it without medical insurance may never receive the support and services they need. Many Occupational Therapists, myself included, do not accept medical insurance because, unfortunately, insurance often doesn't adequately cover the bulk of what we do.

Here are some alternative options. Public schools offer comprehensive evaluations at no cost to families, which can identify and support sensory-related issues affecting the child's classroom performance. Some states offer grants to help cover the costs of therapies. Some Occupational Therapists offer consultative services that can be a more cost-effective way to support your child.

CHAPTER 4
Cognitive Organization

The Vestibular System

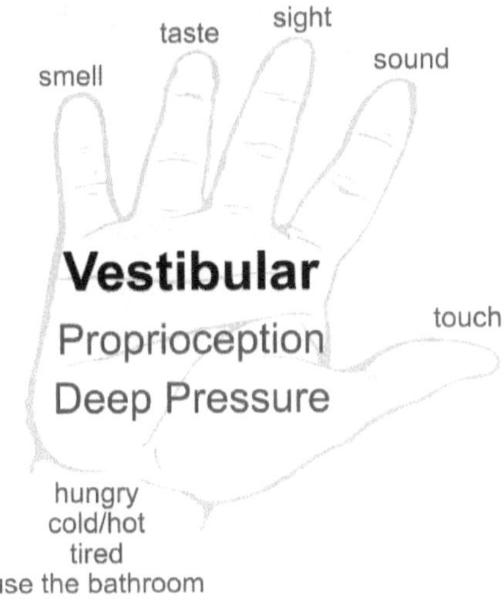

Meet Jackson

It is my distinct pleasure to introduce you to Jackson.

At four years of age, Jackson keeps his round glasses perched perfectly atop his nose and his hair perfectly combed. He organizes his toys and his room in an orderly fashion and thrives in routine. Often described as an old soul because of his witty, mature, and thoughtful nature, Jackson can light up any room he enters.

But there is another side to this sweet boy that is proving very challenging for him and his family. You see, Jackson is a worrier. And it's now to the point his family avoids certain topics around him because it sometimes causes extreme anxiety, leading to struggles both falling and staying asleep.

This worry and anxiety are exacerbated when he encounters change, pretty much of any kind. Changes in his routine, clothes, food, people, or activities can often trigger full-blown meltdowns.

Another struggle for Jackson is that his speech makes him very hard to understand. He has been in speech therapy with only slight progress since he began talking. With ongoing therapy, the hope was that his speech would get better, but instead, his speech challenges have caused him quite a bit of frustration.

As if that were not enough, car rides have also proven to be difficult for Jackson. Whether driving around town or on a family trip, he deals with car sickness, often leading to periods of nausea, headaches, and vomiting. As you can imagine, this spirals the whole family into a tailspin and makes them question taking any future family trips by car.

Jackson's increasing inflexibility and rigid nature are beginning to take a toll on the family, so his mom, at a friend's recommendation, turns to OT for help.

Some groundwork

We'll follow up with Jackson in a little bit, but first, let's start with one of the key components of learning readiness: ***cognitive organization***.

What does it mean to be *cognitively organized*? As previously mentioned, it means your brain can take in new information, process and store it, and have easy access to it for future use.

Let's take a quick look at some fundamental neuroscience. The brain—the main organ of the central nervous system—controls all of the functions in our bodies.[24] Inside the brain, among many other things, are neural pathways. These neural pathways are "a series of connected nerves along which electrical impulses travel in the body."[25] They are formed during the early years of life through a variety of activities, interactions, and movements, including stimulation of our vestibular system.

The *vestibular system* is a vital part of the sensory system responsible for balance and spatial orientation, is increasingly recognized for its influence on cognitive functions, including visuospatial abilities, attention, memory, and executive function.[26]

So what does all of this mean? To simplify things a little, your vestibular system acts like the little air bubble in a level—the tool used to determine if surfaces are even or straight. When we hang a picture, we place a level on top of the frame, and if the little bubble is centered between the two lines, we know the picture is "level." This is essentially how our vestibular system works in our bodies… it is the fluid in our inner ear that tells us if our head is upright.

---

24 "Central Nervous System: The Brain and Spinal Cord." *KidsHealth*, Nemours KidsHealth, 2025, kidshealth.org/en/parents/central-nervous-system.html. Accessed 30 July 2025.

25 "Neural Pathway." *Merriam-Webster.com Dictionary*, Merriam-Webster, 15 July 2025, www.merriam-webster.com/dictionary/neural%20pathway. Accessed 30 July 2025.

26 "Vestibular Dysfunction and Its Association with Cognitive Impairment and Dementia." *Frontiers in Neuroscience*, 2024, https://www.frontiersin.org/journals/neuroscience/articles/10.3389/fnins.2024.1304810/full. Accessed 30 July 2025.

So we have the brain as the main organ of the central nervous system, controlling all the functions of our body, and the vestibular system (part of the brain), responsible for balance and spatial orientation. Now let's take a look at the neurotransmitter ***histamine***. We often think of histamine only in relation to allergies. But histamine not only exists in our allergy system and colon; it is also a neurotransmitter in our brain that helps cells communicate and is crucial to brain function.[27]

In summary, our *brain* controls all of the functions in our bodies. The *vestibular* system is responsible for balance and spatial orientation, and *histamine* helps cells communicate. Now that we have all of the pieces in place, let's talk about cognitive organization using a filing cabinet and a cardboard box as illustrations.

Filing Cabinet vs. Cardboard Box

As we mentioned before, an *organized brain* can effectively and efficiently store, retrieve, and utilize information. Think of your brain as a filing cabinet with neatly labeled files for each brain function. We have a file for math, one for language, one for motor movements, and so on. Histamine, the neurotransmitter, along with its close friend, acetylcholine, travels up and down the neural pathways, storing and retrieving information and keeping things organized.[28] When a child's

> When a child's brain is organized, he has easy access to all the information he has learned.

---

27 Hough, Lindsay B. "Histamine Actions in the Central Nervous System." *Basic Neurochemistry: Molecular, Cellular and Medical Aspects*, edited by G. J. Siegel et al., 6th ed., Lippincott-Raven, 1999, pp. 437–449.

28 Blasco-Fontecilla, H. "Is Histamine and Not Acetylcholine the Missing Link between ADHD and Allergies? Speer Allergic Tension Fatigue Syndrome Re-Visited." *Journal of Clinical Medicine*, vol. 12, no. 16, 2023, article 5350, https://doi.org/10.3390/jcm12165350. Accessed 30 July 2025.

brain is organized in this way, he has easy access to all the information he has learned.

Here is an example. A child is in math class where they are learning addition. 2+2=4. With an organized brain, histamine collects this new information, travels up the neural pathway to the math file, and neatly stores it for future use. The next day in class, the child is asked by the teacher to solve the problem 2 + 2. The neurochemical histamine runs up to the math file and retrieves the answer, quickly delivering it back so the child can easily provide the answer of '4.' This is an example of cognitive organization and efficiency.

Now let's talk about the **disorganized brain**. Instead of having a nicely labeled filing cabinet, this brain looks more like a cluttered cardboard box. The cardboard box is chock full of all the information a person has learned throughout their life, but there are no neatly labeled files. In this brain, histamine works more like a lazy office manager who dumps all of the incoming information into a box to be filed later. But later never happens.

In math class, when a child with a disorganized brain is asked to solve the equation 2+2, they frantically sort through their cardboard box full of all of the information they have ever learned.

"Apples are red."

"THE is spelled T-H-E."

"My dog's name is Spot."

"6! 6 is a number. Is that the one you want?"

Any number of things could happen when this child feels pressure to answer a question they *have* the answer to, but simply cannot find. They may answer with a random nugget of knowledge like, "Did I tell you my dog's name is Spot?" They may sit in a quiet panic, sorting through the entire contents of the cardboard box. Or they may yell out whatever number they come across, even though they know it's not the right answer. The heartbreaking reality is that this child with a disorganized brain, who *has* the answer in his box, may be unable to consistently recall information he had previously mastered. He may be slow to answer simple questions, or he may feel excessive stress with simple tasks.

This type of disorganization can also affect the clarity and organization of his verbal output. It may present as difficulty telling a story with a beginning, middle, and end. Or it may show up as difficult-to-understand speech. Children with disorganized brains often work harder than their organized peers, get negative results, and feel completely overwhelmed.

Even more concerning is that cognitive disorganization can be misunderstood as a low IQ, a learning disability, or a "lazy" child. So often, a child dealing with cognitive disorganization is simply *misunderstood*.

> So often, a child dealing with cognitive disorgani-zation is simply misunder-stood.

As we previously mentioned, cognitive organization is closely linked to the vestibular system. Our vestibular system is the fluid in our inner ear that tells us where our head is in space and whether or not we are upright. Remember, this system is the bubble in the level.

Ideally, this system would be static, self-sufficient, and problem-free, needing little from us to function properly, but that is not the case. It is literally *fluid*. It is not only responsible for balance, motion sickness, and vertigo—it is also a sensory system sensitive to movement, changes in pressure, and changes in internal fluid levels in the body.

So, what happens when our vestibular system is compromised or dysregulated? Think about how you feel when you have congestion, which produces excess fluid in your ears. The excess fluid creates sensations of lightheadedness and the feeling of your head floating. This is the vestibular system's response to the extra fluid. It cannot correctly identify your head's position in space.

So if vestibular regulation in children *is* responsible for cognitive organization (meaning vestibular dysregulation *is* responsible for cognitive disorganization), then what do we do to help children stay regulated and organized? *We let them play!* When stimulated by movements like spinning, swinging, and inversion, the vestibular system activates the histamine in our brains, triggering the establishment of the *cognitive filing cabinet*. Spinning, swinging, and hanging upside down provide many benefits to the human body, but for simplicity, we are going to focus on the organizing

> Spinning, swinging, and hanging upside down are great for our brains!

perks. So don't just let them play, encourage them to play! Teach them that spinning, swinging, and hanging upside down are great for our brains! They are not only organizing their brains, but they are also setting up their filing cabinets! And as we teach our children these vital skills and model them, we are instilling tools that will benefit their mental and physical health for a lifetime.

If you want to test your vestibular system, take a Benadryl. Benadryl is a common allergy medication known as a first-generation antihistamine. A fancy name that means it blocks all histamine throughout our bodies. It blocks histamine in our brains, our allergy systems, and our colons. The stupefied, groggy feeling you get when you take Benadryl is because the bossy neurotransmitter, histamine, has been incapacitated. You definitely would not want to be sitting in math class after a dose of Benadryl, just as you would not want to be sitting in math class with a cardboard box for a brain. Your cardboard box has the exact same information as the child next to you with their nicely labeled filing cabinet, but finding it in your cardboard box will be much more challenging. You are going to work harder and be more exhausted at the end of the day than your friend with a nicely labeled filing cabinet.

> **OT Tip**
>
> *Benadryl crosses the blood-brain barrier (BBB) and blocks histamine throughout our bodies. Antihistamines like Claritin, Zyrtec, and Allegra (second-generation antihistamines) do not cross the blood-brain barrier and can localize to the allergy/immune system; therefore, they have little negative impact on cognitive function. It is essential to talk with your doctor about what medications are best for your child.*

Jackson through a new lens.

Now that you know a little more about the vestibular system and how it works in our bodies, let's reconnect with Jackson. This time, let's take a look through a new lens—a lens of *cognitive organization and vestibular regulation.*

- Jackson organizes his toys and his room in a very orderly manner. *Jackson feels disorganized on the inside, so he responds by being overly controlling on the outside. He keeps his play area and toys neat and tidy to counter his sense of internal disorganization.*

- Jackson does not like any kind of change, nor is he fond of transitions (from one activity/place/environment, etc., to another). *His response to these changes and transitions is to become inflexible and resistant because he instinctively knows that with these changes and transitions comes new informa-*

tion that he must take in, manage, and tolerate. For Jackson, new information is hard to utilize, store, and retrieve, so he would rather avoid the situation altogether.

- Jackson's disorganization is impacting his ability to speak clearly and articulate his thoughts. *Progress in speech therapy is taking longer than expected because his speech challenges are not solely motor in nature. Many of his speech difficulties can be linked to cognitive disorganization.*

- And last but not least is our sweet Jackson's motion sickness, most notably when riding in a car. *Car sickness is a red flag for vestibular dysregulation.*

Even though Jackson was presenting with what appeared to be a number of behavioral, social, and personal issues, we were able to peel back the layers and find that his primary struggle was cognitive disorganization from a dysregulated vestibular system.

Through regular OT work, including a strong focus on vestibular regulation, Jackson developed a sense of internal organization. He began to tolerate changes and transitions with ease and ultimately reached his full potential. His motion sickness resolved, and his speech therapy goals were met more rapidly.

For Jackson's parents, the change was just as dramatic. Because they were able to change the lens through which they viewed their child, they were able to use readiness and regulation as their gauge rather than bad behavior, non-compliance, and big emotions. Instead of trying to calm Jackson down, they provided him with the details and information he needed to tolerate change confidently. They ensured Jackson had enough spinning, swinging, and inversion in his day to set up his brain's filing cabinet. And they helped Jackson discover and use words to describe his overwhelm, rather than show it through resistance and rigidity. Using a new lens of cognitive organization and vestibular regulation, Jackson and his family experienced lasting, transformative changes.

How many other 'Jacksons' are out there?

How many 'Jacksons' have grown into adults who *continue* to struggle with organization and who inaccurately perceive their skills, abilities, gifts, and talents?

The good news is, it is never too late to start implementing tools to regulate our vestibular system. Using these tools will strengthen our vestibular system, help contribute to our overall organization, and lead to a lifetime of purposeful and productive living.

OT Tip

Some Occupational Therapists avoid spinning activities because of the risk of over-excitement. For some children, spinning can be overly exciting and disorganizing, just like Benadryl can cause over-excitement in a small percentage of children. If your child becomes over-excited from spinning, defer to inversion and linear swinging activities (covered in the activities section of this chapter). In my professional experience, the benefits of spinning far outweigh the possible risk of over-excitement. The negative side-effect of over-excitement can be corrected and countered with proprioceptive input, which we will discuss in the next chapter. I use spinning more liberally as an assessment and treatment intervention, but there are many forms of vestibular input to help organize children. It is crucial to work with an OT who is well-versed in sensory regulation to ensure your child is receiving the maximum benefit from their sensory strategies.

Let's organize our brains!

Enhanced cognitive organization is just one of the many benefits of stimulating the vestibular system. Additional benefits include improved balance and body awareness. Some of the best ways to stimulate the vestibular system include spinning, swinging, and inversion (being upside down). In years past, playground equipment such as merry-go-rounds and swings were among the best and most readily available tools for this type of input, but they are not easy to find on playgrounds these days. Luckily, even without merry-go-rounds and swings, we can still develop a healthy vestibular system by intentionally participating in vestibular-rich activities and games.

As with all sensory systems, some people seek input while others avoid it. Vestibular seekers and avoiders both struggle with disorganization. If regulation were viewed as being in the middle, seekers are too far one way, and avoiders are too far the other way. Here are some examples to help identify if your child is a seeker or an avoider.

Seekers	Avoiders
• Seekers love swinging, spinning, and inversion and cannot get enough. • Seekers love amusement park rides. • Seekers love swinging as high as they can. • Seekers are often seen hanging upside down from the couch for long periods.	• Avoiders will shy away from or avoid spinning, swinging, or inversion activities. • Avoiders may shy away from biking, scootering, and activities that require balance. • Avoiders may rush through activities to compensate for their lack of balance. • Avoiders may dislike activities that require them to keep their feet off the ground.

The following are some of my favorite vestibular activities. As you read through these activities, keep in mind the goal is for your child to have regular, routine opportunities for vestibular play, not to complete every vestibular activity to your measure of compliance. A

A child's work is play.

child's work is *play.* These games and activities should be fun! Completing just one or two of these activities each day provides a rich vestibular experience and opportunities to achieve vestibular regulation and cognitive organization.

OT Tip

If your child has an insatiable need for vestibular input (constantly spinning or inverting) or refuses to get on a swing or ride a bike, you may want to contact an Occupational Therapist for additional support. My general rule of thumb is this: It is time to contact an Occupational Therapist if your child's sensory needs or avoidances are disrupting their ability to thoroughly and efficiently perform the tasks that typically 'occupy' their time. For children, these tasks of daily living include but are not limited to learning, playing, and self-care.

Below are a few important notes as you read through these activities.

- Vestibular work is performed to tolerance.

- Too much vestibular work could cause your child to experience overload, which can present as motion sickness: headache, nausea, pale skin, and dark circles under the eyes. If this occurs, you may use rest or proprioceptive (next chapter) input to counter this overload.

- Do frequent check-ins: "Does your tummy hurt? Does your head hurt?" This helps to ensure your child is not approaching vestibular overload.

- Let your child be the guide. They can usually tell when enough is enough.

- Due to the sensitivity of the vestibular system, *encouraging and allowing*, rather than requiring, is key to vestibular activities.

- Always complete these activities with adult supervision and prioritize safety.

Have fun!

ACTIVITIES THAT ORGANIZE

Bats and Butterflies

What you need: Just your children

Bats and Butterflies is the vestibular version of Simon Says. When you say, "Bats," everyone finds a place to be upside down like a bat. Ways to be a bat include:

- hanging their head upside down off the couch

- bending over a chair

- hanging off the monkey bars

- touching their toes

- any safe and creative way of being inverted.

Once everyone is inverted, count to 60 (1 minute). When the minute is up, say, "Switch" or "Butterflies." Then everyone becomes a beautiful, graceful butterfly by spinning carefully in a standing position. Some children may need to be reminded they are graceful butterflies, not moths who recklessly fly around out of control.

If a child feels dizzy, simply stop, then spin in the opposite direction. Let everyone spin to their tolerance for up to 1 minute.

Bats and Butterflies is a fun way to get some vestibular input, and once it is taught, it only takes a couple of minutes to play.

Inverted Ball Push

What you need: A ball. It can be a weighted ball, a basketball, a medicine ball, or any ball that rolls.

Inverted Ball Push is an easy way to invert for an extended period. Two people stand back-to-back and take two steps apart, placing them approximately five feet apart. Both people bend forward and look back at each other between their legs. Once in position, begin rolling a ball back and forth from person to person. Consider using a weighted ball for added heavy work and muscle strengthening.

To make it more engaging, alternate counting as you roll the ball back and forth. You can even count by 2's, 5's, or 10's for added difficulty. Up your game even more by saying the alphabet, alternating letters between each person. And for an even bigger challenge, try spelling words alternating one letter at a time.

For additional strength and motor control work, take one step farther apart after each roll to increase the distance the ball travels.

Inverted Ball Push can provide up to five minutes of inversion, as tolerated by the child.

Inverted Wall Walk

What you need: A timer and a flat, undecorated wall

Inverted Wall Walk is great for inversion and provides upper-body strengthening and joint pressure.

For this activity, have your child stand about a foot away from the wall, with his back to it.

Next, have him bend over and place his hands on the floor, then slowly walk his feet up the wall until he is in a handstand with his arms fully extended and his feet resting against the wall. Once in the correct position, start a timer.

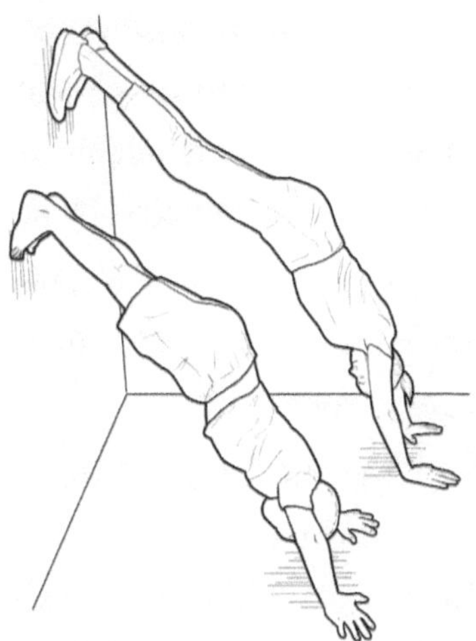

Some children love to watch the timer, so for them, place the timer in a position where they can see it while keeping their head inverted.

Encourage your child to keep his body straight and his head down so he can see the wall between his arms. Encourage him to stay in the position as long as he can. When he feels tired, challenge him to stay up for a few more seconds.

Once his feet hit the floor, stop the timer. Use that time as his baseline, and add 1 second each day until he reaches 60 seconds (1 minute). It is okay to plateau for a few days as the challenge increases, but try not to do less than the previous day. Sixty seconds of inversion is a strong dose of vestibular input. Some children may want to stay up longer than 60 seconds. This may become a family competition. It is acceptable to go longer than 60 seconds because it provides so many additional benefits.

Sixty seconds of *Inverted Wall Walk* each day provides significant vestibular stimulation while strengthening the upper body and providing proprioceptive input (to be discussed in the next chapter).

Side-to-Side Ball Pass

What you need: A ball of your choosing

Side-to-Side Ball Pass is an activity in which two people stand back-to-back and pass a ball to each other from one side, then the other. Each pass should include eye contact between the two people to achieve maximum vestibular input.

I like to use a weighted ball for added upper body strength and heavy work.

For an added challenge, you may also pass the ball over/under. In this same position, passing the ball over the head and then under/ between the legs is another form of vestibular activation.

Passing a ball side to side for up to five minutes is a good source of vestibular input that helps organize our brains.

Front Rolls

What you need: Pillows, if you choose

Front Rolls, also called somersaults, give valuable vestibular input by changing the position of a child's head in space.

To make front rolls more fun, have everyone bring their own pillows. Lay them all out in an open space and let everyone do front rolls on the soft, squishy pillow.

When doing front rolls, it is important to ensure your child's chin is tucked tightly to prevent neck discomfort or injury. "Chin to chest" is the verbal cue to help children remember to tuck their chins before each roll.

Doing 5-10 *Front Rolls* is an easy way to provide organizing vestibular input.

Log Roll Spot It®

What you need: A deck of Spot It® cards

Log Roll Spot It® is a favorite activity for many kids!

Using the card game Spot It®, place half of the cards on the far side of a large room while you keep the other half of the cards with you on the opposite side of the room. Your child will log roll down to the pile of cards, pick one card, and log roll back with it. You may have to encourage your child to keep her body stiff like a log to help her roll in a straight line. When she gets back to you, hold up one Spot It® card and have her locate the matching object on those two cards. When she finds the match, place those two cards aside. Continue having her roll down and back until all the cards have been matched.

For added challenge and a bit of competition, play along with your child and see who can find the match first.

If you do not have a deck of Spot It® cards, try these variations:

- Bingo—the child log rolls down and picks up one Bingo marker at a time until Bingo is achieved.
- Puzzle—the child log rolls down and picks up one puzzle piece at a time until the puzzle is finished.
- If you have more than two people, you can play the whisper game or telephone game. Two people sit on opposite sides of the room. One whispers something in the child's ear, and the child log rolls to the other person and whispers what she heard. The second person says what they heard out loud to see if they heard it correctly.

The motor requirements of *log rolling*, even for just a few minutes, can also help improve your child's body awareness and control, in addition to the vestibular benefits.

Office Chair Target Practice

What you need: An office chair that spins, a wastebasket, and small objects that can be thrown (wadded up paper, bean bags, tennis balls)

Spinning in an office chair provides strong vestibular input.

Place the office chair (make sure it spins) in the middle of the room, away from other furniture. Lower the chair to its lowest setting and have your child sit "crisscross applesauce" in the seat. Using wadded-up pieces of paper, bean bags, tennis balls, or something similar, let him throw the items in the wastebasket while you slowly spin him around in the chair. Keep score and adjust the rotation speed or the distance to the basket to make it more challenging.

Just 1-3 minutes of a spinning game in an office chair provides excellent vestibular input while also developing your child's visual-motor skills and eye-hand coordination.

Inverted TV Show

What you need: A couch and a TV

A wonderful source of vestibular input that many children prefer is hanging your head upside down from the couch while watching a 20-30 minute TV show.

And remember, "encouraging and allowing" are far more important than "requiring" when it comes to sensory input. Your child may want to watch 10 minutes upside down and the rest sitting upright. Children will usually be able to tell when they've had enough.

Blanket Swing

What you need: A blanket and two adults

For children who love to swing, turning a blanket into a swing is a terrific way to provide vestibular input!

Place a sturdy blanket on the floor, and have your child lie "like a hot dog" on it. One adult gathers and lifts the side of the blanket near the child's head, and the other adult gathers and lifts the side of the blanket near the child's feet. When the child is fully and comfortably suspended, swing the blanket back and forth. Your child will be enclosed in the blanket, which provides a hammock-like feel.

Along with vestibular input for your child, the *Blanket Swing* also provides an incredible upper-body workout for adults. Swing the child until you need a break, and then slowly lower them to the ground. Resume when sufficient upper-body strength has returned. Vestibular work should be completed to the child's tolerance, and the *Blanket Swing* can be done to the adult's upper body tolerance.

Inverted Toe Touch

What you need: A timer

Hanging upside down while standing is a great way to provide vestibular input.

For *Inverted Toe Touch*, have your child stand in the middle of the room away from furniture. When you say "Collapse," the child bends at the waist while standing with her legs straight, allowing the top half of her body to dangle, or flop, toward the floor. This position inverts the head. Some children need to be reminded to look at their knees, keep their heads down, or tuck their chins to fully invert their heads.

Once her head is fully inverted, begin the timer and encourage her to stay in that position for up to 60 seconds/one minute.

Inverted Toe Touch also provides an intense stretch for the hamstrings, back, and buttocks, which may be uncomfortable for some children initially. With repetition, most children can overcome the initial discomfort and reap the benefits of improved flexibility.

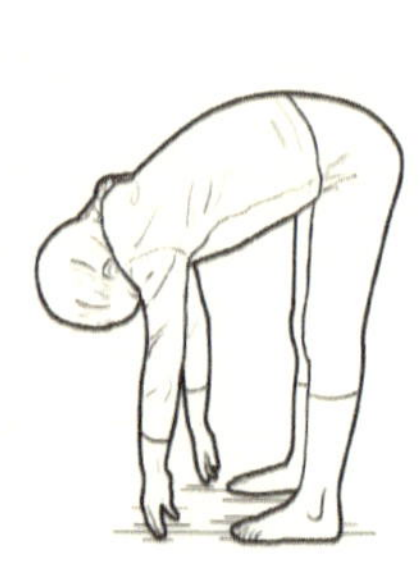
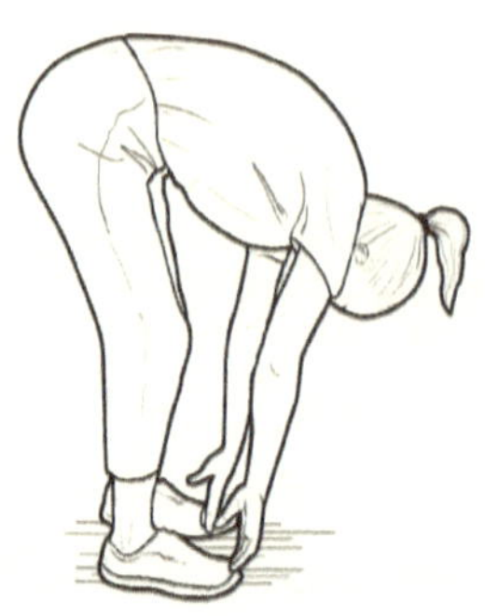

Words of Encouragement

The activities listed above are just a brief sampling of fun and beneficial vestibular activities for children. Once they understand that swinging, spinning, and hanging upside down are beneficial for their overall performance, they usually come up with even more exciting and engaging games and activities to meet their vestibular needs.

When doing vestibular work with children, I am reminded that we were designed for order, not chaos. Our bodies and our minds were perfectly created for our specific purpose here on earth, and when we are not operating at full capacity, we feel out of sorts—kids and adults alike. We need to be cognitively organized to reach our full potential. And for children, that means play with purpose. Children were built to play! Spinning, swinging, and hanging upside down are the types of play that help our children consistently respond to the demands of this world in an organized manner.

> We were designed for order, not chaos.

CHAPTER 5
Physical Calm

The Proprioceptive System

Meet William

William is full of energy! Most days, you can find this six-year-old squatting in a chair, pacing around the room, or standing at the table for meals. He loves any game that involves running, hopping, stomping, pushing, or pulling. William struggles to stay seated for tabletop work in the classroom. My favorite description of William is from his mom. She says he has the sweetest, kindest heart and *the heaviest hands*.

William does everything 'too hard' with those heavy hands.

He colors too hard and breaks crayons.

His high-fives and hugs almost knock you over.

He often breaks toys by banging them too hard.

He plays too roughly and often unintentionally hurts his friends.

His parents and teachers are constantly reminding him to use 'gentle hands,' but it never seems to make a difference. They've tried everything to help him adopt a gentler approach.

Consequences for rough behavior when he breaks a toy or hurts a friend.

Rewards for more gentle behavior when he is able to keep crayons intact, or hug and not tackle.

They haven't been able to find anything to help him with the *heaviness* of his touch. He is getting into trouble more often at school, and his friends are avoiding him at playtime because he is just too rough.

William is struggling with the physical calm of *learning readiness*.

His mom sought help from Occupational Therapy, hoping an OT could help William develop tools and skills to assist with his bull-in-a-china-shop tendencies. What was quickly discovered, in William's case, was a problematic proprioceptive system.

We will catch up with William again later in this chapter, but let's first learn a little about the proprioceptive system and its connection to learning readiness.

The proprioceptive system is one of the most understated sensory systems in the body. When it's working great, no one notices. But when it doesn't work, it's hard not to notice. When this system is not operating optimally, problems arise in many areas of life, as in William's case, where it's affecting his ability to function at home, at school, and in social settings.

The sensory receptors in your tendons, ligaments, and joints make up the proprioceptive system. The job of these receptors is to tell you where your body is in space.[29] With a well-functioning proprioceptive system, you can close your eyes and still know where your body is without seeing it. These receptors provide feedback, letting you know where your body is in relation to its surroundings. For instance, without looking at your body, your proprioceptive system tells you if you're standing or sitting.

It tells you if your legs are crossed.

It lets you know if you're holding something.

It tells you where your hands and arms are.

It's the system that gives us the cues to know how much pressure to apply to a pencil to write our name. Or how tightly we need to grasp a coffee cup to pick it up. Or even how hard to hug someone without hurting them.

---

29 "Proprioception: What It Is, How To Improve It & Disorder." *Cleveland Clinic*, 25 July 2024, https://my.clevelandclinic.org/health/articles/proprioception. Accessed 30 July 2025.

When our proprioceptive system is working well and doing its job, we can move our bodies effortlessly through the world. We know how far away we are from someone else and how much pressure it takes to button a button or tie your shoelaces. When this system is working well, we can also learn motor patterns easily, such as skipping and hopping.

> An optimally functioning proprioceptive system ensures we are physically calm and ready to learn.

An optimally functioning proprioceptive system helps to ensure we are physically calm and *ready to learn*.

But what happens when this system isn't working well? What happens if this system is not regulated? Everything just described becomes more difficult.

It is difficult to move through a space without bumping into others.

We break our pencil lead because we don't know how much pressure is too much.

Learning how to run, skip, or hop is much more challenging.

We cannot show up ready to meet the demands of our day.

People with a faulty proprioceptive system must rely on their other senses to help them decipher the world around them. For example, they will be far more dependent on their visual system to tell them how far they are from someone else. Or they might have to continually touch things to know where they are in relation to them. And because they struggle with tasks that seem relatively easy for most people, those with poorly regulated proprioceptive systems are often labeled as clumsy or uncoordinated. They can become frustrated and are often misunderstood.

While exploring the proprioceptive system and its impact on the sensory system, it is also important to talk about ***serotonin***. Serotonin is a neurochemical that plays a key role in mood, sleep, appetite, and digestion, and is a valuable but lesser-known part of the proprioceptive system. When we receive proprioceptive input through activities such as jumping, hopping, stomping, running, pushing, and pulling, serotonin is released, washing over the body with a feeling of calm.

For avid runners, running is an intense proprioceptive experience that provides a good dose of serotonin through 'pounding the pavement' with their feet. Runners often describe running as an exercise their bodies need or as a way to stay calm through life's challenges. For many, it is a vital part of their mental health, and they often describe the calm as a "runner's high." That "runner's high" is compliments of the neurochemical serotonin.

Now let's apply proprioception and serotonin to the classroom. When a teacher announces it's almost time for recess… or better yet, to get ready for a field trip, the excitement level in the room increases and so does the activity level of the kids. When they get excited, they naturally become more physically active, because physical activity is calming. Kids are jumping up and down, wiggling in their seats, high-fiving their friends, or maybe even rolling around on the floor. All of this activity is releasing the calming neurochemical, serotonin. Sometimes this activity can be misunderstood as the child not following directions or being defiant. And often they lead to time-outs, notes home after repeated instances, discussions of hyperactivity, and, in more extreme cases, the exploration of an ADHD diagnosis.

But what if they simply *can't* sit still? What if they understand what is being asked of them, but their body's need for movement won't allow them to comply?

What if we changed our lens?

What if, for this child, we assumed these were not bad behaviors, but rather the child's body seeking what it desperately *needs*? Instead of the constant requests to sit down, the threat of consequences, or the assumption of bad behavior, what if we tried saying something like this: "Your movement is telling me that you are trying to calm down. Let's try hopping in place for one minute."

Think of it this way. If your child were hungry and asking for food, would you ask them to stop being hungry, or would you give them a reward if they could stop being hungry? Of course not. You would *feed* their *need* for food. In the same vein, we *feed* the *need* for *movement*.

OT Tip

Proprioception is not a system that can be overloaded, unlike the vestibular system, which can be overloaded and reach a point of motion sickness. When children are in constant motion, they are doing what feels good; they are seeking calm, but, on their own, they struggle to achieve what we call "a therapeutic dose." Through OT intervention, we help children reach a therapeutic dose of input. We help the child achieve enough joint pressure so their body no longer constantly seeks it. Research shows the benefits of a moderate dose of proprioception last for up to 2 hours. For children who are heavy proprioceptive seekers, I encourage them to go beyond the point of "enough" and get a bit more input so they can reap the benefits longer. This helps them feel settled and calm longer. For example, if a child is jumping on a mini trampoline and reports getting tired or wanting to stop, I encourage them to jump 20 more times. As they finish those 20 more jumps, I remind them that their body is saying, "Thank you, thank you, thank you!"

William through a lens of readiness

Now let's revisit William. Let's take all we have learned about what it means to be physically calm, how the proprioceptive system tells us where our body is in space, how joint pressure facilitates the release of serotonin, and how all of this works together to help us be ready to learn and apply it to William. Let's now use a lens of readiness, a lens shaped by a regulated proprioceptive system and consistent, therapeutic doses of serotonin, to better understand William and his heavy hands.

We don't often realize how much we use our hands, nor do we have an overall understanding of the pressure we apply in our lives. William is not trying to break the crayon or crack the pencil; he just can't determine the correct level of pressure needed to complete a task. His proprioceptive system can't correctly grade pressure.

He's not trying to hurt his friends by playing too roughly; his proprioceptive system just isn't regulated enough to help him understand what is too much.

When William does things "too hard," we need to feed his proprioceptive system and encourage the release of serotonin by:

- Offering activities filled with joint pressure

- Practicing coloring while teaching the art of grading—light, medium, and dark.

- Grading the pressure of hugs—gentle, medium, and hard—and helping him learn the difference.

- Learning comfortable force with 'high fives,' which is difficult for William to gauge.

William loves playing with others; he wants to be fully present for group activities, and pleasing his adults is important to him. But because his proprioceptive system is giving him inaccurate information about his body's position in space, he stays in constant motion to heighten his body awareness. While this constant motion provides a steady dose of serotonin, which offers William a sense of calm and makes life more tolerable, it does not translate well in a classroom, where movement is often deemed problematic and a distraction to others.

With this new lens, we can see William's need to stay in constant motion for what it really is… his attempt to stay engaged, calm, and present. His attempt to be all the things everyone is asking him to be, but his body has been unable to deliver. Once we help William feed his proprioceptive needs, we can now teach him:

- Which activities help with physical calm
- How to understand what his body is telling him
- Tools that build his confidence in relationships
- Ways to find success in the classroom.

The goal is to set William up for success. To see him for who he is, correctly identifying his struggles and helping him develop ways to feed the needs of his body so that he is ready to learn and ready to engage in a very meaningful way in the classroom.

Through OT intervention, William's mom now has a new lens through which to view her sweet William and his heavy hands. She now understands this need for constant movement as a sensory need, not as bad behavior. And she is able to implement the tools she has learned to feed this need in empowering, rather than punitive, ways.

- She makes sure he gets plenty of proprioceptive activities throughout his day.
- They check in to make sure his needs are met before high-demand activities like school, meals, and playdates.

- She asks questions like, "William, what does your body need before we have to sit down to eat dinner?"
- She uses phrases like, "William, I see your body is trying to stay calm, let's do some more jumping."

Questions and comments like these continue to empower William! He is learning to understand what his body needs and how to best meet those needs. This new lens, along with a small shift in language and intentional joint-pressure activities, has transformed William into a confident child who better understands himself. And he can now ask for what he needs so he can consistently be the *best* William he can be.

As we continue to explore the magnitude of being organized, calm, and connected, we see how vital it is for our bodies to be physically calm in order to be ready to learn. This key to learning readiness is achieved through our proprioceptive system. The rest of this chapter is full of simple activities to help you and your child find new, fun ways to respond to your child's need for physical calm.

ACTIVITIES THAT CALM

Chair push-ups

What you need: a chair with or without arms

Chair push-ups are simply doing push-ups from a seated position. Push your hands on either side of your body into the seat of the chair while suspending your body off the seat. You can push up from the seat or the chair arms.

Have your child hold it as long as they can, then repeat until they report feeling the benefit or have had enough. Count the number of seconds your child can hold the push-up, then increase it by one second each day. Over time, notice how your child becomes more regulated **and** develops improved upper-body/upper-extremity strength.

If you don't have a chair, you can also do these push-ups from a seated position on the floor. Solid surfaces are easier to push off of than softer surfaces, so push-ups on a kitchen chair will be easier than on a couch or sofa cushion.

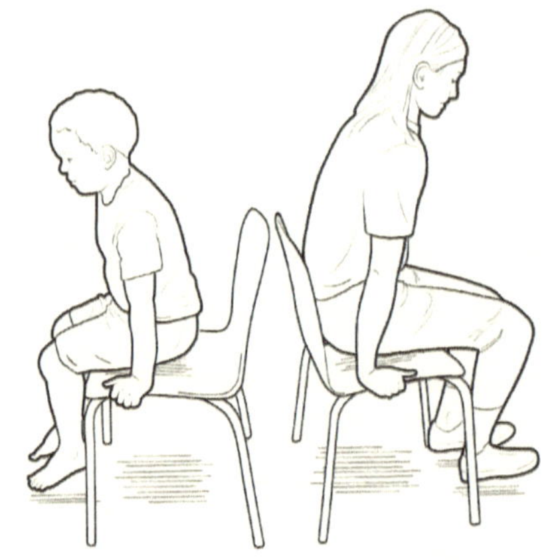

Mini trampoline

What you need: a mini trampoline

A mini trampoline is the foundation of many fun and entertaining activities that benefit the proprioceptive system. Mini trampolines often come with detachable counters to count jumps or minutes spent jumping.

Some children like to jump every day and try to beat their record from the day before. They measure this either by increasing the number of jumps or the number of minutes jumped.

It is also fun to toss a small ball or bean bag back and forth with your child while they are jumping. When they have mastered tossing and catching one bean bag, add a second bean bag for an additional challenge. This activity resembles basic juggling as you each throw a bean bag to the other at the same time. An added benefit of this activity is its positive effect on visual-motor development.

Another option is to play a target game or shoot balls in a basket while jumping on the trampoline. This is great multi-tasking practice! And for an added bonus, keeping track of points strengthens number awareness, working memory, and math skills.

To add upper-body strengthening and visual tracking support, stand on opposite sides of the trampoline and bounce a weighted ball back and forth between you.

Your child can practice spelling words, math facts, or study for a test while they are jumping on a trampoline. Incorporating a trampoline into studying can add a little fun to otherwise boring homework. Learning in motion improves recall while meeting your child's needs.

> ## Safety tip
>
> *Always set up your trampoline in an open space. Position it away from sharp corners, edges, and fragile decor. Children with proprioceptive struggles often have poor body awareness, which makes it challenging for them to stay on a trampoline. When you first set up the mini trampoline, assess your child's ability to stay in the middle of the equipment while jumping. If they are not able to consistently stay in the middle (or struggle with falling off) of the trampoline, stay next to the trampoline to "spot" them until they are skilled enough to jump without your near support.*

Weighted ball

What you need: A weighted ball.

I recommend soft weighted yoga/pilates balls instead of a medicine ball.

When selecting a weighted ball for your child, I recommend purchasing one that is the weight in pounds your child is years old. For example, if you have a five-year-old child, then a 5-pound ball is appropriate. Some heavy sensory-seeking children may be able to tolerate 1 pound more. So, you may get a 6-pound ball for a five-year-old child. Once your child reaches a 10-pound ball, I don't recommend anything heavier. As your child ages, continue to use the 10-pound ball.

Weighted balls can be used for *catching/throwing*. For an additional challenge, you can count the number of throws and increase it by one throw every day.

Weighted ball slams are a wonderful option for joint pressure. Simply raise the ball above your shoulders and slam it down on the ground as hard as you can. This is a favorite of many kids! Always offer a challenge similar to the following:

- Do you think you can do ten ball slams today?

- If you do ten ball slams, I'll do ten.

- Let's each slam a ball at the same time and see how many we can do together.

Weighted ball bowling is another fun activity. Small or medium-sized bowling pins are placed across the room at an adequate distance for your child's age and strength. Then simply roll the ball across the floor and knock them down! As an added challenge, keep score. You now have your very own proprioceptive and sensory-friendly bowling alley!

For safety reasons, never use the hand-held metal/steel weights with children.

Animal walks

What you need: just your child

A great way to provide proprioceptive input is to have your child practice motor patterns like bear walks, frog jumps, and crab walks.

Bear walks:

- Your child walks on all fours, keeping their legs and arms straight.

Frog jumps:

- Your child squats on the floor with their fingers lightly touching the ground inside of their legs.

- Next, they jump up and forward across the floor, returning to the squatted position between jumps.

Crab walks:

- Your child leans back and places their hands on the ground behind them while keeping their bottom off the ground.

- Next, they walk their legs and arms forward across the floor.

- Added challenge: Have your child try walking sideways like a real crab.

- Need an additional challenge? Place a small bean bag on their tummy and see if they can keep moving while keeping it there.

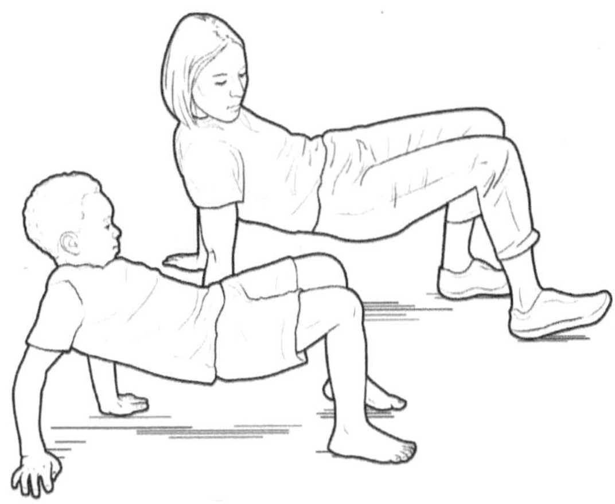

Get creative! Take turns naming different animals, then create a motor movement that resembles how you think that animal might walk. Examples include but are not limited to:

- Snakes—slither across the floor

- Squirrel—scurry across the floor
- Elephant—lumber across the floor.

Hopping in place for 60 seconds

What you need: just your child

Children love to hop! Even without a trampoline, children love to hop. And did we mention… children love to hop!

With just 60 seconds of hopping in place, your child's proprioceptive system receives valuable regulating input. If your child can't hop for the full 60 seconds, simply time how long they can hop and add a second a day until they reach the full 60 seconds. Always set 60 seconds as your goal. This can be done anywhere and at any time. You can have them hop in place while waiting in line, in a hotel room, or on the back deck.

Running laps

What you need: just your child

As we previously mentioned, running is a great proprioceptive activity. The "pounding of the pavement" provides strong input.

Go for a run with your child through the neighborhood in the morning before school. Some children find a path through the house to create a lap and use it for indoor running, or they can simply run laps around the outside of the house. Whatever course they choose, continue to build in challenges through the number of laps or the number of minutes they run. Running is an easy way to add intentional input into your child's proprioceptive system.

Proprioceptive movement is calming for children. With these activities and our new lens, we can help children organize their brains through vestibular input and calm their bodies through proprioceptive activities.

Equally as remarkable is the type of input children need to feel socially connected. Social connection comes from deep pressure. In the next chapter, a little boy named Joseph will help us better understand the link between social connection, hugs, and learning readiness.

CHAPTER 6

Social Connection

"How good and pleasant it is when brothers live together in unity."
(Psalm 133:1)

The Deep Pressure System

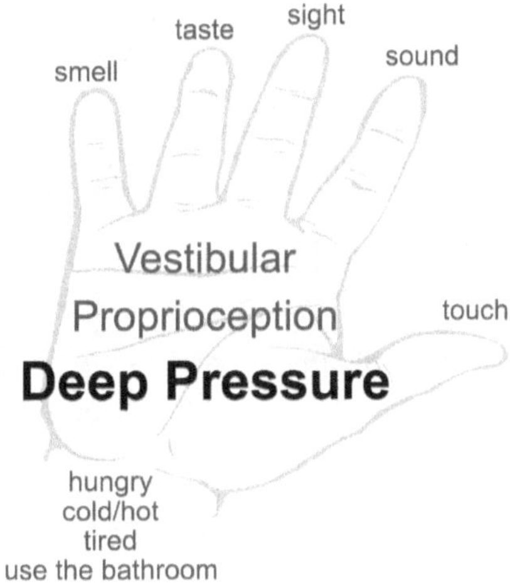

Meet Joseph

Joseph's preschool teacher asked me to come and watch him at recess. She reported Joseph spends most of recess going down the slide and purposely throwing himself belly-first into the mulch. Sure enough, when I arrived to observe, Joseph was repeatedly going down the slide and then free-falling face-first into the mulch. He would get up with the biggest smile on his face and do it all over again with an intensity and precision that suggested he was performing the most important work of his life. Four-year-old Joseph *was* doing important work. He was taking care of his sensory needs. Without the deep pressure of these crashes, Joseph struggled to socially connect with his teachers and peers. He had a hard time making eye contact and often sat alone in the classroom. Joseph was very smart and knew a lot about many things, but he struggled to stay engaged in classroom conversations or group activities. His teacher knew he had far more potential than she saw each day and felt that his unusual playground behavior might provide some insight into his underperformance in the classroom. She was right.

The keen eye of Joseph's teacher was a critical key to understanding Joseph's struggles.

First, let's do a little recap on the kids we have met so far.

In Chapter 2, we met Mac. Mac is four years old. He enters the room like a tornado, leaving a trail of his things behind him. He runs and trips on his way to the play area, snatches a toy from sweet Sadie, accidentally knocks over his best little friend, Charlie, and struggles in the classroom.

In Chapter 2, we also met Sam. Sam is 14 years old, gets A's & B's, has trouble being prepared for class, often loses things, stands during class, is constantly chewing gum, and bites his nails and pencils.

In Chapter 4, we met Jackson. Jackson is four years old, wears round glasses, is a bit of an old soul, overorganizes his toys and room, thrives on routine, lights up a room, and is a worrier.

And in Chapter 5, we met William. William is six years old, full of energy, typically stands at the table during meals, is always on the move, plays too roughly with his friends, has a kind heart, and has heavy hands.

But what do we know about Joseph? Much of our introduction to Joseph describes him as struggling with eye contact, not engaging with other kids, often sitting alone, and spending most of recess crashing into the mulch at the end of the slide.

Of significance is how much of a presence the other children have, compared to Joseph, who struggles to be seen at all in the classroom and among his peers.

Joseph is underperforming in the classroom and not meeting his full potential because he is not ready to learn. His behavior suggests he is socially disconnected. We know there is a lot more to learn about Joseph, but we don't get the opportunity to see into who he really is because he seems withdrawn. To Joseph, his daily work of caring for and protecting his sensory system is all he can manage. And that leaves little room for the social connection that would show us there is a beautifully funny, clever, and delightful little boy in there. We may not be able to see to the heart of who Joseph is right now... but we will soon.

As we begin to explore social connection, let's first think about what it feels like to be hugged. Think about the best hug you've ever had. And think about what and how your body responded once the person released you from their embrace.

How did you feel?

It could be peaceful. Maybe emotionally connected to them. Maybe safe.

What did you experience?

Your heart rate may have decreased. Maybe your body felt relaxed.

In contrast, consider how you feel when someone you don't like or respect brushes by you, or wants to engage with you.

How do you feel?

Maybe slightly agitated or grumpy. Maybe angry. Or maybe… nothing.

What do you experience?

Maybe apathy, or your heart rate increased. Maybe you're numb, or you felt the blood pulsing through your veins.

I use these two examples to allow you to fully experience the benefits of social connection. Social connection means we feel connected enough to someone else that their thoughts, opinions, and feelings matter. Without social connection, it is difficult to learn, build meaningful relationships, and facilitate behavioral change.[30]

Imagine, for a minute, trying to learn from someone with whom you have no connection. And then imagine the same learning experience with someone whom you respect and admire.

Feeling a connection to others is a shared responsibility. The speaker's responsibility is to be easy to connect to, and my responsibility is to have the capacity for connection. The same is true for our children. Social connection is two-sided. Our children's responsibility is to show up with the capacity for connection. Their teacher's responsibility is to be relatable. When we send a child to school without the capacity for connection, the richness of their learning experience is negatively impacted.

So, how do we achieve a sense of social connection?

---

30   Jethani, Zara. "The Neuroscience of Love and Connection." *Pacific Neuroscience Institute*, 5 Feb. 2025, https://www.pacificneuroscienceinstitute. org/blog/brain-health/the-neuroscience-of-love-and-connection/. Accessed 30 July 2025.

By activating the connection neurochemical, *dopamine*.[31]

What activates dopamine?

Deep pressure.

The ***social connection*** we receive from deep pressure is the third element of learning readiness. When our bodies receive deep pressure through our skin and muscles, like in a hug, dopamine is released, which makes us feel connected to each other. When we experience deep *social connection*, dopamine levels surge, creating a sense of euphoria similar to the effects of addictive substances like cocaine.[32]

Just as histamine has a partner, acetylcholine, dopamine has a partner, ***oxytocin***. Oxytocin works in conjunction with other neurotransmitters like dopamine to create the positive feelings associated with social interactions and strong relationships.[33] I include this simply to note that many complex factors and neurochemicals are at play when we work to achieve a state of cognitive organization, physical calm, and social connectedness. As with all the complex systems in the human body, it is easy to get bogged down in the details, so we are going to streamline our conversation to the three main

31 Mount Sinai Health System. "First-in-Human Study Reveals Dopamine and Serotonin Have Overlapping yet Distinctive Roles That Influence Social Behavior." *Mount Sinai*, 2024, https://www.mountsinai.org/about/newsroom/2024/first-in-human-study-reveals-dopamine-and-serotonin-have-overlapping-yet-distinctive-roles-that-influence-social-behavior. Accessed 16 Nov. 2025.

32 Goldman, Bruce. "Addictive Potential of Social Media, Explained." *Stanford Medicine News Center*, 29 Oct. 2021, https://med.stanford.edu/news/insights/2021/10/addictive-potential-of-social-media-explained.html. Accessed 30 July 2025.

33 Lancaster, Mac E., and Ran D. Anbar. "How Oxytocin Affects Our Relationships." *Psychology Today*, 30 Mar. 2024, https://www.psychologytoday.com/us/blog/understanding-hypnosis/202402/how-oxytocin-affects-our-relationships. Accessed 30 July 2025.

players in the neurochemical regulation game: *histamine, serotonin,* and *dopamine.*

We hug each other not just because it's a social norm, but also because it makes our bodies feel socially connected to the other person. Human-to-human contact is one of the best forms of social connection. For the self-proclaimed "non-huggers," human-to-object contact works well too. Weighted blankets, pressure clothes, and massagers are all ways to get deep pressure in the absence of human contact.

> Human-to-human contact is one of the best forms of social connection.

Let's now insert the COVID-19 pandemic, which normalized social distancing and no-contact measures. A pandemic that encouraged us not to touch, hug, shake hands, or high-five each other. The very thing we as human beings need to feel connected was discouraged and frowned upon. Still today, we reconsider whether we are going to shake hands when we meet someone new, or high-five in celebration. It has impacted our social connection. It has impacted our children's sense of social connection.

This is the best time to address the false sense of connection we get from screen time, particularly from social media. During the pandemic, our children's screen time and screen use increased dramatically. Remote learning was primarily driven by screen use. We used screens to entertain our children while we worked from home.

Research has shown that "dopamine levels are overall higher when people interact with another human as opposed to a computer."[34]

---

34 Mount Sinai Health System. "First-in-Human Study Reveals Dopamine and Serotonin Have Overlapping yet Distinctive Roles That Influence Social Behavior." *Mount Sinai,* 2024, https://www.mountsinai.org/about/newsroom/2024/first-in-human-study-reveals-dopamine-and-serotonin-have-overlapping-yet-distinctive-roles-that-influence-social-behavior. Accessed 16 Nov. 2025.

Social media platforms can trigger a dopamine release, but the effects may differ from those of real-life social interactions. While social media can provide a sense of connection and novelty, excessive use can lead to an overstimulation of the reward system, potentially contributing to addiction and other negative consequences. This explains how and why we can feel irritable after extended time scrolling. The experience is literally impacting us at a neurochemical level. It also supports the importance of getting our dopamine the authentic way—through human-to-human interaction.

Isn't it interesting now, when you think about children who are touching other people all the time? A child who is touching everybody and everything, giving hugs, trying to pick up their friends, or throwing themselves down on the floor is seeking social connection. Their bodies are telling them they need dopamine to feel connected.

When we view them as a child with self-control issues and use rewards and consequences to try to change their behavior, we not only *misunderstand* the child, but, just as unfortunate, we teach the child to misunderstand themselves. This child inaccurately sees themselves as a problem or as poorly behaved, rather than as a child seeking social connection. Instead of viewing these kids as unable to keep their hands to themselves or as too touchy, we can now see them as children who need social connection.

This small change in our parenting lens offers a dramatic opportunity to support healthy, accurate self-perception in our children.

As we have already learned, any sensory system can be out of sync through either seeking or avoiding (aka. hyper/hypo, high/low arousal), and the deep pressure system is no different. Both seeking and avoiding are problematic for children. They are both considered a state of dysregulation.

Joseph is a seeker.

He needs deep pressure and searches for ways to meet this need. However, some children avoid physical contact and don't want to be touched. They get irritable when they're touched. They run away from grandparents who just want to hug and kiss them. They may use behavior or sharp words to let others know they don't like physical contact. They tend to be *misunderstood* as difficult and ill-tempered when in reality, they are just protecting their sensitivity to deep touch.

> They tend to be misunderstood as difficult and ill-tempered when in reality, they are just protecting their sensitivity to deep touch.

Whether the child is seeking or avoiding deep touch, our goal is that their sense of deep pressure is regulated enough they feel connected to others and value what others think, do, and say. This sense of social connection allows children to participate to their fullest potential in a learning environment. So, let's take a look at Joseph and see how we were able to help meet his sensory-seeking needs and, as a result, allow him to show up as his best self to the demands of the classroom.

Joseph's big grin at the end of each mulch crash let us know crashing felt good to his body. He needed deep pressure through his skin and muscles to tolerate the social demands of the classroom. And that's just what he did. He *tolerated* it. He was not thriving, engaging, or participating. He was simply tolerating being in school. With regular OT sessions, Joseph was able to get enough deep pressure through resistive tunnel crawls, weighted-ball massages, and crash pad crashes (explained at the end of this chapter) to meet his sensory-seeking needs and flood his system with dopamine. Joseph was then able to return to class and engage with his friends, participate in group discussions, and answer questions when called on. We began to see Joseph's precious sense of humor through his clever comments and playful interactions. Joseph's whole personality began to shine, and his peers rushed to be around him to learn what he had to share. Because his deep-pressure needs were met, Joseph could play with his peers at recess and participate in games and group activities.

Joseph's parents learned and practiced exercises that helped Joseph feel connected to others. They were able to understand and unlock Joseph's true potential.

Deep pressure helps us feel socially connected by releasing dopamine, which promotes engagement with others and social success in the world around us.

As we mentioned at the beginning of this chapter, being socially connected is the third pillar of learning readiness. Along with cognitive organization and physical calm, social connection allows us to thrive and successfully fulfill our calling and careers here on earth. Each of these pillars is achieved through movement and sensory input, accentuating the value of keeping our children active and in motion throughout each day.

Here is a list of deep-pressure activities for you and your children to enjoy at home. Doing these activities with your children ultimately helps them discover ways to successfully meet these needs on their own.

ACTIVITIES THAT CONNECT

Weighted Ball Massage

What you need: a soft weighted ball of the child's choosing. As mentioned in the previous chapter, we recommend a weighted ball that is the number of pounds the child is years old. A 5-pound ball would be appropriate for a five-year-old child.

Weighted Ball Massage. Have your child lie on their tummy, face down on a rug or carpet with their arms extended straight out to their side, and their legs extended straight down. Slowly roll the weighted ball over their back, legs, arms, hands, and feet. Avoid their head, neck, and buttocks. Check in with the child frequently to ensure the pressure is just right. Avoid playful tickling during this activity. Stop when the child indicates they are done.

Let the child then roll the weighted ball over your back, arms, legs, hands, and feet while you model enjoying the massage and asking to stop when you have had enough.

Family Sandwich

What you need: 3 family members

Family Sandwich is stacking people on top of each other in a prone position. Start by having Dad lie face down on the floor. On top of him, have your sensory dysregulated child lie facedown. Finally, Mom lies facedown on top of the child. Each person makes sure the person below them has plenty of breathing space, and their nose and face are not covered or blocked. Each person lies down slowly, ensuring they do not harm the person below them. And when anyone asks to stop, everyone promptly, carefully, and safely gets up and discontinues the sandwich.

Family Sandwich can be made with any combination of family members and is always made to everyone's tolerance.

Couch Cushion Squish

What you need: two couch cushions

Couch Cushion Squish is making a couch cushion sandwich with your sensory-challenged child. Place one couch cushion on the floor, and have your child lie belly-down on it. Then place the second couch cushion on top of your child, like the second piece of bread of a sandwich. Ask your child if that is enough pressure or if 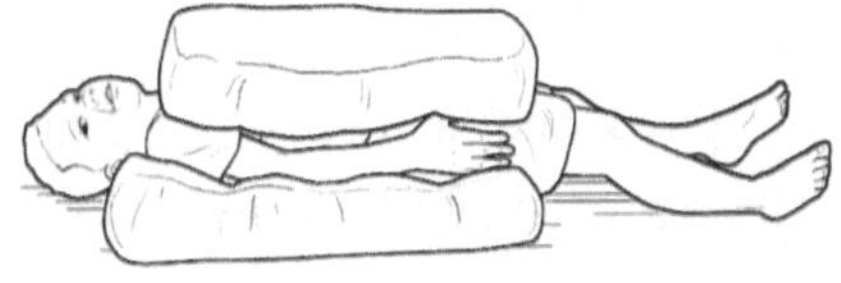 they'd like you to add pressure to the top cushion to squish them more tightly. They may want you to push, lean, or sit on the cushion to add more deep pressure. All pressure should be given to the child's tolerance. When they ask to stop the activity, promptly comply.

Burrito Wrap

What you need: a blanket or a towel

Burrito Wrap is wrapping your child tightly up in a blanket or towel. Lay the blanket or towel out on the floor. Have your child lie prone on one edge, with their head off the blanket. Have your child grab the edge of the blanket and slowly log- 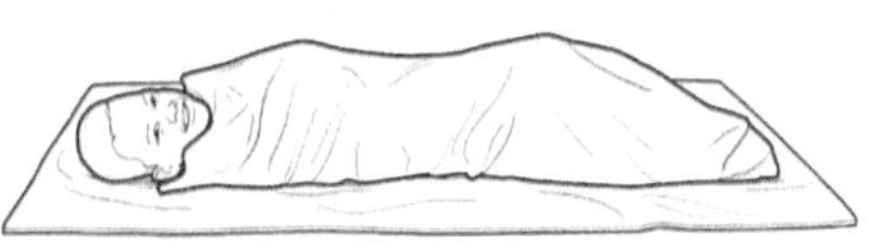 roll across it, rolling up in it like a burrito. The child's head starts off the blanket, so their face never gets completely covered up. As the child rolls, continue to ensure their face and head remain uncovered and unobstructed. Let them stay inside the burrito as long as they prefer, and when they are done, help them slowly unroll out of it.

Hugs

What you need: you and your child

Hugs are one of the best sources of deep pressure and a dopamine release. Have fun with your hugs.

Ask your child to identify if you are giving a gentle, medium, or hard hug. Also, have your child give you hugs to decipher if they are giving a gentle, medium, or hard hug.

Hug through an entire favorite song.

If your child is sensitive to human-to-human contact, teach them to give a self-hug by encouraging them to wrap their arms around their back and try to touch their hands together.

Use a timer to time the hug to help your child recognize what they need and what they can and can't tolerate.

Massages

What you need: you and your child

Massages include any deep pressure given through the skin and muscles. Some people like deep massages, others prefer gentle touch. Experiment and help your child determine their preference.

If your child doesn't like human-to-human contact, you can use a rolling pin, a tennis ball, or any object your child selects.

When massaging a child, **exclude** the tummy, chest, and buttocks. **Avoid** the sides of the torso and **avoid** tickling them.

The key to a successful massage is meeting the child's needs and preferences. When you talk with your child about their preferences, it not only helps you better understand how to meet their needs, but it also helps the child become aware of their needs and practice asking and advocating for themselves.

Weighted blankets

What you need: a weighted blanket.

The suggested fitting is 10% of the child's full body weight. Example: a 60-pound child will typically benefit from a 6-pound blanket. Note: Some children will prefer a heavier blanket; for them, you can use 10% of their body weight plus 1 pound. Example: an 80-pound child can use a 9-pound weighted blanket (10% or 8 pounds, plus 1 pound). Other children may want a lighter weight, which is also acceptable.

Weighted Blankets are an easy way for children to get deep pressure input. Your child can rest under a weighted blanket during quiet time. They can use a weighted blanket to help them fall asleep at night. Some children like to walk around with their weighted blanket draped over their shoulders like a cape. Let them be creative in the ways they use their weighted blanket. You may find that their blanket becomes a great source of comfort for your child.

Pressure Clothes

What you need: breathable clothing, a size too small

Pressure Clothes are tight enough to give your child a gentle, all-day-long hug. When you go online to search for pressure clothes, you will find therapeutic pressure vests that are effective, but overpriced. They often come with a wearing schedule. Always follow the product's or professional's recommendations when using such tools.

A more cost-effective option might be to buy a breathable shirt (Under Armour® has great options), a size too small that your child can wear under their clothes or even as their shirt. Fitted swim shirts also provide a nice level of deep pressure input throughout the day for your child.

Pillow Fights

What you need: pillows

Pillow Fights are a fun and easy way to get and receive deep pressure.

To make the experience more enjoyable for everyone, each person can set the pressure they want, and then it is up to the others to ensure they provide that level. Dad might request hard pressure, Mom might request light pressure, and sister might want medium pressure.

To make the experience more contained, you may have only two family members play, with them taking turns swinging the pillow at each other.

You may choose to time the activity or limit the number of contacts to provide another level of predictability.

Pillow fights, in and of themselves, run the risk of getting out of control. Know your family. If you don't feel your family can tolerate a pillow fight without injuries and tears, skip this one and use one of the other strategies.

Resistive Tunnel Crawl

What you need: a resistive tunnel or tubing

A *Resistive Tunnel* is a breathable fabric tunnel or tube through which children can crawl. Children enjoy crawling through them, resting quietly in them, and even being swung in them by two adults holding either end.

In the same vein, body socks provide a nice level of deep pressure and can be easily purchased on many websites, including Amazon.

Body Crashes

What you need: a large crash pad

Body Crashes are an opportunity for your child to belly flop, jump, or crash onto a large crash pad, pillow, or bean bag. My favorite crash pad is a Big Joe FUF®, but any fluffy soft pad will work. You will want to set up the safety parameters allowed in your home and have your children verbalize and demonstrate their understanding of the rules. Some often-used parameters include:

No head-first crashing; you must protect your neck

One person on the crash pad at a time to prevent being landed on or crashed into

No free-air flips onto the crash pad

We have covered a lot of information so far. It is okay to feel a bit overwhelmed. Please hang in there and remember why you picked up this book in the first place. Parenting is hard, and it challenges us to our very core. You are reading this book because you want to do things differently, to do better for you and your family. This is all new. It is challenging what you think, what you believe, and how you have functioned as a parent. When we learn new information, it is common to feel like we have more questions than answers. Now is a good time to stop and answer some questions about learning readiness. Join us in the next chapter, as we tackle some of the most commonly asked questions.

CHAPTER 7
More Questions Than Answers

Now that we have covered being *organized, calm, and connected*, the *vestibular, proprioceptive, and deep pressure systems*, and *histamine, serotonin, and dopamine*, there is a very real possibility you have more questions than answers. If you are like me, when I learn new information, it produces a multitude of questions. It makes me wonder how it relates to my family and situation, or how I might actually implement this into my daily life. This information may also be both enlightening and confusing. Or it makes sense to you, but you struggle to explain it to your spouse and parents/grandparents.

The next few pages will help answer questions, clarify points, or simply build confidence in all that you have learned so far. Remember, this parenting thing is not a destination. It's a journey. One that you and your child are on together. Remember to give grace… to them and to yourself. The learning process can be fun! I have seen so many families go from struggling and feeling hopeless to reconnecting and thriving! As you read through the questions, give yourself the space to learn as you go. No one ever knows it all, and most of the fun is in the process.

Question #1:

This all makes sense, but what if my child isn't excitable? What if they are only disorganized?

It is possible for a child to be all three, just one, or maybe two. Everybody's sensory profile is slightly different... and constantly fluctuating. And because our sensory system is a "fluctuating and changing" system, one's profile can shift and change over a lifetime, during growth spurts, or even throughout the same day.

Question #2

How can I quickly and easily recognize disorganization? Excitability? Disconnection?

Common signs of cognitive disorganization include:

- Having a hard time telling a story with a beginning, middle, and end
- Purposeless play
- Garbled speech

Common signs of physical excitability:

- Can't sit still
- Always on the go—running, jumping, pushing, pulling
- Pacing
- Restless leg; constant leg movement while sitting
- Constant fidgeting

Common signs of disconnection:

- Low eye contact
- Avoids social interactions

- Low interest in social experiences
- Withdrawn or shy

Question #3

How do I know the order in which to do the exercises?

No matter the specific readiness challenge, it works best to organize the brain first, then calm the body. Deep pressure is always icing on the cake. Doing all three in this order is the best starting place.

1) Vestibular

2) Proprioception

3) Deep pressure

Another reason you want to provide proprioceptive input *after* vestibular input is if you ever overload the vestibular system and your child shows signs of motion sickness (pale skin, dark circles, headache, nausea), the serotonin released from proprioception can calm and ease the symptoms of motion sickness.

This reminds me of the time my sister did aerial yoga at a spa in Arizona. She called me right after the class and said, "Oh my gosh, I am so motion sick from hanging upside down while swinging from the suspended fabric!" I told her to give herself joint pressure (proprioceptive input) through chair push-ups, wall push-ups, and interlacing her fingers over her head and pushing down. I think she thought I was nuts, but she gave it a try. She called me later on to share her shock and disbelief that it actually worked! She said she even went back to the yoga studio and told the teacher, if in the future, other students get sick from their aerial yoga class (vestibular input), to have them give themselves proprioceptive input to calm their motion sickness.

As you become more familiar with the activities and which ones work best for your child's specific symptoms, you will become more comfortable using them with greater flexibility. For example, you may choose to use the trampoline before dinner because it helps your child sit calmly in their chair throughout the meal. Or you may use inverted wall walk before studying for a test to take advantage of the histamine benefits of storing data in the brain in an organized manner. As you become more comfortable, I encourage you to be creative and have fun with these activities and exercises.

Question #4

Vestibular overload sounds like car sickness. Are there any strategies that work for car sickness?

Yes, vestibular overload is the same as car sickness. Proprioceptive input helps counteract motion sickness from car rides. You can stop the car and do a few of these exercises to help relieve your child's symptoms. Have your child do push-ups, take a walk around the car, or interlace their fingers and press down on their head to help calm symptoms of overload. Unfortunately, if they have to return to the car, they will most likely overload again due to the ongoing vestibular input from the car ride.

Other strategies that we have found that work to prevent car sickness include:

- Having your child face forward and watch the road ahead. (This excludes infants who are recommended to be rear-facing.)

- Never look at a book or screen when the car is in motion.

- Use your hands as "blinders" to block input from your peripheral vision.

Question #5

How do I select the right exercises for my child?

All movement is good, but intentional regulating movement is great!

Show your child this list of exercises and encourage them to select one from each category to make their body feel better. If they are unable to make a selection, tell them to simply try one and then discuss how it made their body feel.

HANG (Vestibular)	HOP (Proprioception)	HUG (Deep Pressure)
Inverted Wall Walk	Mini Trampoline	Squishing between pillows/cushions
Bats and Butterflies	Wrist/Ankle weights	Pillow fights
Spinning—office chair	Weighted Ball	Burrito Wrap
Over/Under ball pass	Hopping Up/Down Stairs	Wrap Up Tightly in a towel
Inverted ball push	Running Laps	Pressure Clothes
Rolling—log, front	Carry Heavy Objects/Groceries	Resistive Tunnels
Swinging - blanket swings	Gum	Body Socks
Outdoor swings	Stomping, Pushing, Pulling	Family Sandwich
Merry-go-round	Jump Rope	Deep Massage
Inverted wall walk	Punching Bag	Catch with Weighted Pillow

Exercise selection should be guided by your child.

It should **NOT** be treated as homework or a To Do list. Instead, it should be viewed as self-care; things we do to take care of our needs. Things we do to prepare our bodies so we can perform to our fullest potential.

A child's work is play. These activities and exercises have to be fun. Every child's idea of fun is different. Once they understand why they are doing them, how to accomplish them, and what their bodies need, most children come up with better, more creative activities than most adults. For example, as long as your proprioceptive-seeking child is achieving a good dose of joint pressure through the activity they have created... let them! There is no one best way to receive this input; there is only the best for your child.

A child-favorite activity is to set up an obstacle course that includes activities from each area—vestibular, proprioception, and deep pressure. Children love to set up obstacle courses; they love it when you set up obstacle courses for them, and they love it if you complete the courses they have designed.

Question #6

When should I do these exercises with my child?

Learning readiness work should be done *before* a demand is placed on a child. Whether the demand is homework, mealtime, or quiet time, readiness activities should happen first. These exercises are often called a Sensory Diet because, like food, our bodies need a steady supply of them.

If a child is in the middle of a demand and shuts down, your only responsibility is to keep them safe. *Trying to get your overloaded child or a child in shutdown to jump on a trampoline or touch their toes will not work and will most likely make the situation worse.*

Question #7

How often should we do these exercises?

A good rule of thumb is 2-3 times a day. Once before school and once after school. Sometimes people use a version of these strategies to aid with bedtime (we will discuss sleep later in Chapter 9).

Question #8

Sensory overload sounds like a fight-or-flight response. Is it?

Sensory overload is very similar to the fight-or-flight response. When our sensory system has taken in as much as it can handle and becomes overloaded, it is very common for children to fight, flee, or shut down. To protect themselves, they may become aggressive, yell, or hit. They may run to escape the sensory stimulation. And they might even shut down, becoming nonverbal, unresponsive, or unengaged.

In these moments, our natural tendency is often to try to reason with the child or further explain what we need from them. Talking to or explaining things to a child in a state of sensory overload is ineffective and usually detrimental. They will not be able to comprehend what you are saying. Your words may agitate them, worsening the situation. When a child is in sensory overload, your only job is to keep them safe.

When your child comes out of the sensory overload, I recommend letting them rejoin the family activity without addressing the incident at that moment. They were just in overload, and, like in fight-or-flight, they won't have an accurate recollection of what just happened. Secondly, immediately after an overload is a tender time when they are at greater risk of cycling back into overload. They just need the time and opportunity to return to something normal. In an hour or two, or maybe even the next day, when they are more regulated, you can talk about what happened using a lens of regulation. Asking questions like:

- Was there anything I could have done differently to help you during that tough moment?
- Could you feel any signs that your body was heading into that difficult time?
- What can we plan to do next time to make situations like that less difficult for you and your sensory system?

I recommend you have a ***"Put Yourself Back Together"*** place in your home. This is different from a time-out spot and should have no association with it. A time-out is a potent behavior modification strategy. It serves an entirely different purpose and is quite effective in changing a child's behavior. Sensory overload is not a chosen behavior.

In Chapter 9, we will explore the difference between behavior and regulation in more detail.

A *"Put Yourself Back Together"* space is a place where your child can go to help their sensory system settle. It might be a little tent in the corner of their room that has a weighted blanket, a soft toy, a snack, a drink of water, a fidget, a book, headphones, or soft music. A child can go there on their own accord, or you may come up with a code word you say if you notice your child is approaching overload. Practice using the code word during times when the child is regulated so they understand it is a measure of self-care, not a consequence for bad behavior. A child should not be "sent" to their *"Put Yourself Back Together"* space. Children are "sent" to time-out. The *"Put Yourself Back Together"* space is a safe place for your child to go, where they can regroup and eventually rejoin the activity without consequences. The *"Put Yourself Back Together"* space should also be separate from their general play area. It is a cherished sanctuary of self-care and safety. Let your child take an active role in designing their *"Put*

Yourself Back Together" space and its contents. Some children like to give it a name that represents a sense of calm and protection. Get creative and enjoy the planning and setting up of this space with your child.

Question #9

What is the relationship between integrating and regulating senses?

This is such a good question. As mentioned before, it is easiest to think of the integrating senses as our learning senses—the ones that take in information from the world. Our regulating senses determine how ready and able we are to receive and process information. Our integrating, regulating, and interoceptive senses are tightly woven together and make up our sensory system. They function independently yet relationally. When you look at the three sensory areas—integrating, regulating, and interoceptive senses—it is essential to understand your child's entire sensory profile. In what areas are they hypersensitive, and in what areas are they hyposensitive? Once their entire profile is determined, you can outline a treatment plan. I have found the best way to settle sensitivity in the integrating or interoceptive senses is to treat the regulating senses and educate. The neurochemical benefits of histamine, serotonin, and dopamine settle a plethora of integrating and interoceptive problems. Combined with education on how to accommodate the sensitivities when they are problematic, you can facilitate a very successful outcome for your child.

Question #10

What is the relationship between food and the sensory system?

Eating food is arguably one of the richest sensory experiences humans have. It is also one of the most complex acts in which we participate. Many children are challenged by food and the task of eating, because exploring and consuming food requires all five integrating senses. Eating involves seeing, smelling, hearing, touching, and tasting the food.

If your child is struggling with the sensory experience of eating, ask them what the food looks like. What do they think of when they touch it? Is there anything that stands out to them about how the food smells? These types of questions will help you better understand the food experience through your child's eyes.

You may also help your child categorize their food preferences into Foods They Eat, Foods They Are Interested In, and Foods They Definitely Don't Want To Try. Then, make available and begin to slowly expose them to the foods on their 'Interested In' list.

Food is a basic need. As parents, we often measure our success by our ability to meet our children's basic needs. Having a young eater with strong preferences and dislikes can sometimes trigger an emotional response in us. We begin to overly celebrate food trials or shame food refusals. I caution you to keep your emotions in check with food challenges. A simple reminder is, "don't emote at the dinner table." As adults, no one celebrates when you finish your mashed potatoes, and we have to respond the same way with our children. Begin by simply making foods available to your children, encouraging them to explore the food and discussing its sensory characteristics, and the experiences they are having with it.

> Don't emote at the dinner table.

Eating is not only impacted by our sensory system, it also requires a well-functioning motor system. Successful eating can be hindered by the physiology of our mouth, the size of our tonsils, or the severity of a tongue tie. When your child is struggling with food and eating, and you feel you have exhausted all the tools in your parenting toolbox, you may choose to seek professional support to uncover the cause of the struggle. Some commonly trained professionals include your pediatrician, a speech therapist specializing in swallowing, an occupational therapist specializing in sensory-related food issues, a dietitian, or a feeding therapist.

Question #11

How do I find an OT who treats sensory issues?

A common mistake parents make is assuming all Occupational Therapists have the same training. I made that same assumption when I entered the workforce. But after working with a variety of therapists, I realized we all have different areas of expertise and different passions. When you are looking for an Occupational Therapist with expertise in sensory regulation, you want to ask the following questions:

- What is your specific training in sensory processing disorder?
    - SIPT certification, Dunn's Model of Sensory Processing, Ayres' Sensory Integration, Sensory Modulation Model, and sensory training with Julia Harper are all great training programs
- How many years have you worked with children with sensory processing issues?
    - I recommend a therapist with at least five years of experience with sensory issues. Or having a therapist who works closely with, or is supervised by, another well-trained therapist is also a good option.
- What is your favorite problem area to treat?
    - You are looking for a therapist who enjoys treating sensory regulation issues. If their favorite treatment area is, for example, handwriting, positioning, or splinting, they may not be the best fit for your child's sensory needs.
- How do you assess sensory issues?

- Common assessment tools are the Sensory Profile 2, the Sensory Processing Measure-2, and the Ayres' Sensory Integration and Praxis Test (SIPT).
- What sensory equipment do you have in your clinic?
  - You are looking for a clinic that has swings, crash pads, spinning equipment, monkey bars, trampolines, and tunnels.

These questions and answers are intended to bring clarity and peace to some of your sensory concerns. We have discussed sensory regulation, inside and out, and have equipped you with a number of tools and tips to help better understand your child through the lens of learning readiness. When children are ready to learn, it is easy to teach them new skills.

In the next chapter, we will examine skills related to group membership. In many areas of our lives, we are required to function within groups. Group membership skills are necessary for classrooms, sports teams, meetings, and group projects. It takes a level of awareness of group membership to attend family events, drive down the road, and live in a civilized society. We need to know how to function in a group successfully to board a plane, attend a concert, or play in a band. There are many skills that contribute to a successful group experience, but we will focus on the top three group membership skills that impact your child's success in the classroom.

CHAPTER 8
Group Membership and Social Skills

When you choose to send your child to school, you are choosing to put them in a group learning environment. Group learning environments are characterized by frequent, ongoing group learning, project learning, and peer interactions. Considering that your child will be in school for anywhere between 12 and 19 years of their first 25 years of life, it seems consequential to be intentional about teaching them group membership skills. And when you consider we are designed to live in community for our entire lifespan, group membership skills become even more paramount.

In "What is a Group?" Mark Smith references the following definitions of a group.

We mean by a group a number of persons who communicate with one another often over a span of time, and who are few enough so that each person is able to communicate with all the others, not at second-hand, through other people, but face-to-face. *George Homans (1950: 1)*

To put it simply, they are units composed of two or more persons who come into contact for a purpose and who consider the contact meaningful. *Theodore M. Mills (1967: 2)*

A group is a collection of individuals who have relations to one another that make them interdependent to some significant degree. As so defined, the term *group* refers to a class of social entities having in common the property of interdependence among their constituent members. *Dorwin Cartwright and Alvin Zander (1968: 46)*

A group exists when two or more people define themselves as members of it and when its existence is recognized by at least one other. *Rupert Brown (1988: 2-3)*[35]

As parents, keeping these definitions in mind helps us see the importance of preparing our children *for* group membership and *with* group membership skills. From the first day of school to youth group to almost every job we will be asked to do, understanding what it means to be part of a group is vital for success. Being an empathetic, perceptive, and emotionally sound group member is a coveted skill and one of the few things AI has yet to master. That's because group membership is one of the things that makes us *human*. Strong group membership skills enhance human success at all levels, and it is far easier to teach a four-year-old group membership skills than it is to teach them to a 14-year-old. This is where we would confidently use the old adage, 'the sooner, the better.'

---

35 Smith, Mark K. "What Is a Group?" *The Encyclopedia of Pedagogy and Informal Education*, 2008, updated 2018, www.infed.org/mobi/what-is-a-group/. Accessed 20 Apr. 2025.

When you think about what it takes to be in a group, many skills come to mind. However, over my years supporting children in classroom settings, I have identified three skills that are vital. If you can send your child to school with these three skills, consider it a gift to your child's teacher, to your child's academic success, and the learning environment as a whole.

These skills are ***being a first-time listener, being able to hold a thought,*** and ***being able to wait without entertainment.***

Mastering these skills will not only set your child up for success in the classroom but also group membership success for years to come.

First-Time Listening

In my early years of pediatric occupational therapy, I worked with an amazing preschool teacher, Amy Stadler, whose classroom was a model for group membership success. Her students were engaged, loved learning, loved school, and were kind to each other. Her classroom had a noticeable calm. I became intrigued by the workings of her classroom and found myself frequently stopping in to study the intricacies and nuances of her success. Amy's classroom was the first place I heard the phrase *first-time listening*. She would often compliment students for being good first-time listeners. She modeled first-time listening and taught it with great detail to her group of children. It became apparent that this one simple skill was foundational to the success of her classroom, so I quickly added it to my parenting and OT Toolboxes.

Being a first-time listener means you respond appropriately the first time a request is placed on you. With effective first-time listening, the person making the

> Being a first-time listener means you respond appropriately the first time a request is placed on you.

request doesn't have to repeat themselves, raise their voice, or become emotional.

When a child comes to school without the skill of first-time listening, teachers must frequently repeat their instructions, focus on redirecting, and ultimately lose valuable instruction time. When several children in a classroom are unable to be first-time listeners, the learning environment can become quite chaotic.

Here are a few things you can do at home to partner with your child's school to develop your child's first-time listening skills. Spend an entire month focusing on, teaching, practicing, and mastering this new skill. Luckily, life presents a multitude of teachable moments in our home environments.

- Hold a family meeting to discuss what first-time listening is and what it looks like, and role-model it.
  - *Don't fret, a family meeting doesn't require a boardroom. Many family meetings occur in the car. Some occur while going on a walk. A family meeting can occur anytime all the necessary family members are together. Ideally, it would be the entire family together at one time, but if that rarely happens, make the best of it and maybe hold two family meetings on the same topic. Having one of the older children or your spouse run one of the meetings is also a great option. As families, we make space and time for what is important.*

In this family meeting, ask whether anyone knows what the term "first-time listening" means. Ask if they know anyone who is a great first-time listener. Have your child ask you to do something, and then model what first-time listening looks like. It is also important to model what it doesn't look like. Have some fun! Practice with low-risk, single-step tasks.

- Please push in your chair.

- Please hang up your coat.

Take turns making the request and responding to the request. Have them make observations about the request. Observations might include,

"Oh, you are not yelling."

"You only asked once."

"You didn't get angry."

- Use the language "first-time listening" in your home. Use phrases like, "Thank you, that was great first-time listening," or "I'm going to ask you to do something new, please listen to all the details and be a first-time listener." Normalize the term "first-time listener" in your home.

- Intentionally practice first-time listening.
  - *Always gain their attention first. If your child is engaged in another activity, they will need to discontinue it and give you their undivided attention during the practice. Getting them to stop their current activity doesn't count as practicing first-time listening, because for many children, stopping one task and starting another (transitioning) is challenging in and of itself.*

Say to your child, "We are going to practice first-time listening. In my regular voice, I am going to ask you to do something, and then you will respond appropriately the first time. "Let's try it. Sam, please put your cup in the sink." When Sam puts his cup in the sink, he gets a high five for being a first-time listener. Do this exercise as many times as needed, with as many different tasks as needed, until your child masters the skill without you raising your voice, repeating yourself, or becoming emotional.

Once your child masters a single-step direction, then give them a two-step direction and work up to a three-step direction.

- At the end of each week, share with your child a few of the times you saw or experienced them being a first-time listener, and let them know how much you appreciate them working on this skill with you.

When your child becomes a first-time listener, it not only creates a better learning environment in the classroom, it will also improve your home life!

Holding A Thought

> Holding a thought is a conversational skill that elevates and enriches social interactions.

Holding a thought is the ability to hold a thought until the appropriate time to speak it. The opposite of holding a thought is blurting, interrupting, and calling out. When several children in a classroom are unable to hold a thought, class discussions are fragmented, and teaching energy is spent managing verbal balance. But when you send a child to school who has mastered this skill, it allows all voices to be heard. It gives space for class discussions to flow and for high-quality teaching and learning to occur. When started early, children as young as four or five can practice and succeed at holding a thought.

Holding a thought is about timing, not about silencing. It is a conversational skill that elevates and enriches social interactions.

Of note, in Chapter 4, we discussed the disorganized brain, which is like a cluttered cardboard box rather than a neatly organized file cabinet. Well, imagine having that cardboard box full of everything you know and everything you have ever learned. You have searched and finally found the one thing in the cardboard box you want to share with others—the story about your puppy licking your ice cream cone last night. To you, it is the best story ever, and you really, really want to share it! You know if you don't share it in this very instant, it will just fall back into the abyss of the cluttered cardboard box. It will be really hard to find again, and you might even forget about it. Your urgency to tell that story is so elevated you might start flailing your arm back and forth and making noises as if the story is going to pop right out of your mouth. Your eyes get all sparkly, and your facial expression exudes energy and excitement. You might just succumb to all of the pent-up energy and blurt out the story!

This disorganized child risks being misunderstood as a noncompliant child who is having difficulty holding a thought. In reality, they are simply doing their best to stay engaged and participate. This offers just a glimpse into the importance of learning readiness before we place any significant demands on a child.

Here are a few things you can do at home to help your child learn the skill of holding a thought. For an entire month, focus on developing this one skill. Only work on one skill a month. It is too confusing and much less successful when you teach and practice the development of too many group membership skills at the same time.

- Sit down with your child and spend time talking about the importance of holding a thought, what it means, and role-playing how it works.

- Use the following language in your home:

  "Holding a thought,"

  "Please hold your thought."

  "You did a great job holding your thought!"

- Practice holding a thought at dinner. Start a conversation asking everyone to share the most exciting thing that occurred that day… and you go first. Make sure your child can wait their turn to speak—*hold their thought*. Every night, you go first, and your stories get longer and longer to help your child extend the time they can hold their thoughts. Keep in mind, in morning circle time, when each child is given the opportunity to share, the last child must hold their thought while all of the other students share - sometimes that could be 20 or more kids!

- Verbally acknowledge when your child is observed holding a thought!

- At the end of every week, recognize your child for working on this skill. Share all the times you witnessed them holding their thought and let them know you are proud of their efforts.

Enjoy watching your child develop the skill of holding a thought and reap the benefits as your family conversations become richer and more inclusive!

Unentertained Waiting

Being able to wait without entertainment is a lost art. Before phones, tablets, and the glorification of busyness, people would just wait. They would stand in an elevator and just wait. They would stand in line at the grocery store and wait. People would sit in a doctor's office waiting room and just… wait. Waiting without entertainment used to be built in moments of regulation, times of reflection, or quiet pauses. Today, whether we are waiting for the doctor, in a grocery line, at the airport, or using a public restroom, we can find endless entertainment at our fingertips thanks to the popularity of smartphones. We are in a constant state of stimulation, but in a school setting, there are countless requirements and opportunities to wait without being entertained.

For many children, the first time they are given the opportunity to wait without entertainment is in a school setting. Throughout the day, children are expected to wait in line to go to recess, to lunch, to specials, to ask their teacher a question, and to complete their work. What makes this kind of waiting different is that there is nothing and no one to entertain them. At school, they simply have to wait.

For children who can wait unentertained, these waiting periods can be quick, easy, and effortless. But when there are children in the class who have not mastered this skill, these waiting periods are disruptive, disorganized, and can even risk the safety and well-being of others. I have seen children wander off in search of entertainment. I have seen children invade their friends' personal space in search of entertainment. And I have seen children not listen to their adults while pursuing entertainment. It can be chaotic.

> For children who can wait unentertained, waiting periods can be quick, easy, and effortless.

Because children need to be able to wait without entertainment in the school environment, it is valuable to spend a month with your family focused on developing this skill.

At home, you can:

- Discuss the importance of unentertained waiting and why children in schools and groups need to master this skill.

- Use the language "unentertained waiting" and "waiting without entertainment" in your home. Normalize it.

- Model unentertained waiting. This is a hard one! In today's world, it feels uncomfortable and awkward not to be busy, especially in public. But for your children's sake, try it. Get on an elevator and just stand there. In a waiting room, just sit.

Wait in a grocery store checkout line without glancing at your phone or grabbing a magazine. With time, you will begin to appreciate the built-in pause. The time to think. The peace and quiet.

- Practice unentertained waiting. Tell your children you are going to the grocery store to practice unentertained waiting. Take your entire list and all your children, and shop for all your groceries. When you approach the checkout lines, get in the longest line and tell your children you all will be practicing waiting without entertainment. No one will have access to a phone, tablet, book, snack, or any source of outside stimulation. And then remind them they have something far more entertaining than any of those things—they have their brains. When we are not feeding our brains constant stimulation and information, our brains are free to create, think, design, and invent. Tell them you can't wait to hear what they did with their amazing brains when you get through checkout. After checkout, discuss what their brains had time to think about!

- Verbally acknowledge when your children do a great job waiting without entertainment!

- At the end of every week, talk with your children about all the times you saw them able to wait without entertainment, and encourage them to continue extending the length of time they can wait unentertained.

Throughout the month, you will enjoy watching your child develop the skill of waiting without entertainment and seeing the beauty of your child's creative thoughts and ideas. As you teach this skill, you will transform waiting into a peaceful time rather than a stressful one spent trying to manage your child's expectations and entertainment! And even more powerful, you will gift your child's classroom with calm transitions.

Once your child masters these three crucial group membership skills, here are a few more that, when acquired, will make your child an elite group member.

- *Recognizing a Voice of Authority*—one must be able to recognize and appropriately respond to the voice in charge. The voice that directs and guides the group.

- *Squaring to the Speaker*—for others to understand you are speaking to them or for you to show you are listening to others—one must know to square their body to face the person to whom you are speaking or the person who is speaking to you.

- *Voice Volume*—to be heard without overpowering, one must understand and utilize a voice volume easily tolerable to others.

- *Being an active listener*—to sustain an ongoing conversation, one must show interest, ask questions, and use appropriate body language to indicate reciprocity in communication.

- *Bodily Functions*—one must easily and readily recognize and refrain from bodily functions deemed appropriate for various settings. Some bodily functions may be acceptable at home but not in public settings.

- *Endurance*—adequate physical endurance is required to successfully participate in group activities to be able to maintain focus and engagement in the group task or conversation.

- *Perseverance/Stick-to-itiveness*—group decision-making and membership both require each individual to have a degree of perseverance. One must possess the ability to exercise patience, social awareness, and respect.

- *Core Strength*—core strength allows one to sit in a stabilized position so their body isn't distracting themselves or others; it also allows distal muscle groups to work and engage with ease, enabling one to execute fine motor tasks and activities.

Now that we understand the value of group membership skills and have the tools to teach them, let's elucidate the power of social skills. Childhood is where we learn, practice, and begin to master socialization. Historically, children developed social skills by spending endless hours with peers, same-aged friends, and relatives. With the increased isolation and speed at which we live, children no longer have the luxury of extended time with limited adult intervention to try out and develop social skills. Let's further explore social development and ways to enrich your child's interpersonal skills.

Social Skill Development

Do you catch yourself on repeat with comments like, "You all need to take turns!" or "Come on, guys, you gotta share!" or "Hey, hey, hey, we don't use unkind words in our house!"

Have you ever wondered why you have to say the same thing over and over again? Or, why you are having a hard time moving the dial with the development of these seemingly simple skills?

Skills like taking turns, sharing, and using kind talk fall under the category of social skills.

Seeing your child find social success is one of the most heart-warming experiences we can feel as parents. To be honest, knowing they have a good friend, watching them lovingly care for another, or seeing them interact well with an adult are some of our proudest parent moments. On the flip side, seeing our child struggle to make friends, defend themselves

> Seeing your child find social success is one of the most heart-warming experiences we can feel as parents.

when spoken to unkindly, or be excluded or rejected by other children in a group are among the most heart-wrenching parenting moments. It is not that we want our children to be the most popular, the most admired, or the most socially savvy child in the group, but we long for our children to have friends and be equipped to manage themselves in social settings.

The development and acquisition of social skills are well researched and well documented. One of my favorite go-tos is Judith Coucouvanis's book, *Super Skills*.[36] Judith's book lays out social skills in a logical manner, offers a plethora of activities, and provides an assessment checklist. As the expanded book title (*A Social Skills Group Program for Children with Asperger Syndrome, High-Functioning Autism and Related Challenges*) suggests, Judith has written this for children on the autism spectrum. However, in my practice, I find this checklist useful for all children. Every child needs to learn how to socialize, and they need an organized approach to learning social skills. In my opinion, this book is not just for children who have a diagnosis that includes social challenges or delays; it is for all children.

Historically, children learned and developed social skills by being put in social situations. They were expected to pick up social skills by observing others or maybe even by osmosis. We didn't put much thought into how children learned to socialize. But for today's children, the isolation caused by the pandemic and the increased use of screens has led to a bit of a social skills pandemic of its own. We are seeing more and more children, especially typically developing children and children without social skill-related diagnoses, with weak or absent social skills. More children need a structured, intentional

---

36 Coucouvanis, Judith A. *Super Skills: A Social Skills Group Program for Children with Asperger Syndrome, High-Functioning Autism, and Related Challenges.* 1st ed., Future Horizons, 2005.

social skills development plan, and I have found Judith's *Super Skills* book to be an effective tool. It offers an easy-to-digest perspective on social skill development.

She breaks down social skills into four categories. Fundamental Skills, Social Initiation Skills, Social Response Skills, and Getting Along with Others. Here are a few skills that fall under each category.

Social Skill Development Judith Coucouvanis			
Fundamental Skills	**Social Initiation Skills**	**Social Response Skills**	**Getting Along With Others**
Eye Contact	Inviting Some-one To Play	Listening	Taking Turns
Correct Voice Volume	Joining In	Following Directions	Sharing
Timing	Asking For Help	Waiting	Playing By The Rules
Correct Voice Tone	Using A Person's Name	Staying On Topic	Using Kind Talk

Fundamental Skills are the starting place. They are the skills that allow you to enter the social setting; the social game, if you will. Fundamental skills include eye contact, appropriate volume, response timing, and tone of voice. Having these skills equips you to begin to consider a social interaction.

Once you have solid fundamental skills, you are now able to initiate social interactions. Social initiation includes skills such as inviting someone to play, joining an activity with others, asking for help, and using a person's name when talking to them. These are the skills required to begin social interactions. They are the first point of contact in socializing.

From there, you can then respond to social interactions by being able to listen, follow directions, wait, and stay on topic. Response skills keep the conversation going. They acknowledge the other person's impact and presence in the social dynamic. They are what allow social interaction to maintain or even deepen.

Once you have developed fundamental skills, can initiate social interactions, and respond well in social settings, you have all the tools needed for Getting Along With Others. Getting Along With Others skills are high-level social skills that bring it all together. They are skills such as taking turns, playing by the rules, sharing, and using kind words. These are the skills by which others judge one's social competence. These skills are included on many report cards. They often translate to the level of success achieved in group projects and team leadership roles. They are linked to how others perceive your character and social integrity. As one friend said, "They are the skills that get you hired and fired." They are important.

So, if these are such necessary skills, then why is it so hard to master them? Why are we, as parents, having to constantly remind our otherwise intelligent children to use kind words or share?

If you are in constant reminder mode or find yourself repeating, "I need you all to share," in your sleep, it may be time to stop and ask yourself: *What skills are missing that are preventing my child from mastering this particular Getting Along With Others skill?*

If my child is struggling with a Getting Along With Others skill, then which fundamental, initiating, or responding skill is missing? If your child were going to learn the skill by constant reminders from you, then, based on the number of those reminders you have provided, the skill should have been easily mastered.

So, let's change the lens.

Instead of saying they are struggling with sharing, let's step back and assess if they may be struggling with *asking for help, listening, or waiting*. If waiting is the missing skill, then when that is further developed, your child can begin to work on sharing with a much higher chance of success and mastery… and less reminding and repeating on your part.

Structured Playdates

Having a structured playdate is a great way to develop and practice social skills. Most people never really think about the format of a playdate. In a structured playdate, find a parent-child duo willing to participate in a highly organized, 30-minute playdate. The playdate will be at your house and will include a simple 30-minute activity to help your child work on one skill. It will set your child up to experience playdate success. It is crucial that the playdate is only 30 minutes or less. Even if it is going well, you will want to stop after 30 minutes. If you already have a child who is not finding success in the playdate arena, keeping track of time allows the child to end on a high note, increasing the chances that everyone will want another playdate.

You will tell the other parent in advance what the activity is and your goal. They agree to drop off their child and pick them up 30 minutes later.

The activity might be making a bead bracelet, and your child's goal is to learn three new things about their friend. You might even give them the questions to ask.

What is your favorite color?

Do you have a pet? If so, what is its name?

What is your favorite treat?

After the playdate is over, you review with your child what they found to be successful and unsuccessful, and have them recall and tell you the answers to the three questions they asked their friend. Learning about others and listening to their responses are necessary skills for playdates. This type of playdate focuses on one skill and sets your child up for success with learning how to listen.

Another activity might be having a friend over with three different activities from which to choose. The goal for this playdate is for your child to let someone else choose the activity and then play it with enthusiasm, good participation, and without complaining. Again, using the structured playdate model, this environment allows your child to practice flexibility, tolerate others taking the lead, and learn to play a game they didn't select... all valuable skills in successful playdates.

Another idea might be having a friend over to play a board game, with the goals of helping your child be a good sport, encouraging their friend if they are losing, and celebrating their friend if they win. Playing fair and being a good sport are invaluable skills for successful playdates.

As you can see, by setting up a structured playdate and keeping the other parent fully informed, you are intentionally teaching your child social skills one skill at a time. This technique helps your child learn the skills they need to succeed in small-group settings.

Additional note: During these structured playdates, stay focused on only one skill. As parents, we will want to comment on all the skills our child is lacking. Commenting on all their weak skills takes away focus from the success of a single skill. In the first example, when the child is learning to ask questions and listen while making a bracelet, we could make the playdate less impactful by peppering the child with additional comments, such as "Make sure to clean up." "Let your friend pick their beads first." "Try not to make a mess." "Oh, isn't their shirt so cute?" You get the point. Stay back, let your child work on the skill of asking and listening, and you can set up other playdates to work on the other skills… one at a time.

Organized Sports

> Preschool-aged children typically lack the skills necessary to succeed in team-sports.

We can't really talk about group membership skills and social skill development without mentioning organized sports. Over the last 30 years, the entry age for organized sports has dropped to as young as 3-4 years old for some children.[37] The problem with starting organized sports this young is that preschool-aged children typically lack the skills necessary to succeed in a team-sport setting. They are still figuring out basic social skills and generally don't have the cognitive capacity to understand the complexities of team sports, including membership, offense, defense, and strategy. When we put them in a complex sports setting, we are forgoing their opportunity to learn the foundational skills necessary to step onto a court or field successfully. They may look like they are playing the sport, but in reality, they are simply doing what they are told. They are not employing the higher-level thinking required to play the sport successfully.

So, I caution you to think long and hard before placing your preschooler on an organized sports team. Human development is sequential and predictable. Each skill builds off the one before it. A

---

37 Gutierrez, Patrick. "Organized Sports: How Young Is Too Young?" *Baltimore's Child*, 1 Apr. 2017, https://www.baltimoreschild.com/organized-sports-how-young-is-too-young/. Accessed 30 July 2025.

child walks before they run. We babble before we talk. Socially, we have to be aware of ourselves before we can be aware of others.

After watching so many preschool-aged children struggle in organized sports, I really want to start a program called Disorganized Sports. In Disorganized Sports, children would come into a space with a variety of balls—big, small, heavy, and light. Children would learn that big balls move more slowly than small balls, and that it hurts more when you drop a heavy ball on your toe than when you drop a light one. Children would be given space to explore, play, try, fail, and plan. Preschool children need the opportunity to experience play in this way. Those are the foundational skills that will enable them, as an older child, to be a successful member of a sports team. So yes, I am discouraging organized sports for preschool-aged children.

However, until I get this Disorganized Sports program up and running, if you are inclined to put your preschooler in organized sports, vet the program well. Ask questions like:

What level of competition is embedded in the program and instilled in the children?

What are the goals of the program? Winning or learning?

What is the experience of the coaches with preschool-aged children?

What disciplinary method do they use with the children?

What other skills are being *intentionally* taught in the practices? Sportsmanship? Sharing? Endurance? Attention?

We now have a framework and some tools to develop social and group membership skills. Even when our child is well-equipped socially, it can sometimes be challenging to distinguish between behavior and regulation. In Chapter 9, we are going to tease out the difference between behavior and regulation and add some new tools to our Parenting Toolbox.

CHAPTER 9
Behavior and Sensory Regulation

"Don't let anyone look down on you because you are young, but set an example for the believers in speech, in conduct, in love, in faith and in purity."
(1 Timothy 4:12)

Behavior and Sensory Regulation

Maybe your child's behavior isn't the problem; maybe it's the answer. So often we see all unwanted behavior as bad behavior, but what if that is not the case? What if our child's behavior is a window into their state of regulation? How can we sort out what is bad behavior from what is sensory dysregulation? Here are some insights that might help us better understand the differences between the two.

There is definitely a difference between bad behavior and sensory dysregulation. It isn't always a crystal-clear difference, but there is one.

Bad behavior is an action within the child's control, motivated by wanting something or by wanting to get their way.

Sensory dysregulation is an action beyond the child's control; it arises from overload or overstimulation and is motivated by self-preservation and need.

Where it can get convoluted is when a child unintentionally uses bad behavior to signal that their sensory system is in overload.

An example of this is when Tyler hits Seth because Seth is sitting too close to him. Tyler didn't hit out of intentional anger or a desire to harm Seth. Tyler's sensory system was being overwhelmed by Seth's nearness. Tyler was beginning to feel a sense of overload, but didn't yet have the words to explain it, so he hit Seth to create distance, which is essentially taking care of his sensory system in an act of self-preservation.

Or, what about when Walker pushes Savannah because Savannah won't stop singing loudly?

Like Tyler, Walker is experiencing overload, but from Savannah's loud singing. He may have asked Savannah to stop once or given a mean glare, but Walker isn't yet able to explain the physical pain his ears are experiencing, so pushing Savannah helps terminate the singing and protects his sensory system. Walker didn't push from a place of anger or intention to harm, but from a place of self-preservation.

Our typical go-to response is to tell Tyler, "We don't hit!" and to tell Walker, "We don't push our friends." Both of which are behavior-modification responses, meaning we assumed bad behavior. For most of us, the main tool in our Parenting Toolbox is behavior modification.

> Before we simply assume behavior, look for patterns.

We can adjust that lens by asking a few questions first. Before we simply assume behavior, look for patterns.

Does Tyler not like hugs?

Does he usually get upset in crowded spaces?

Do clothing tags bother him?

If the answer to any of these questions is yes, we can help Tyler learn a new way to respond when people get too close to him. We can teach Tyler to get up and move away, ask for more space, or ask an adult for help. These are all "instead of" choices he can make when tolerating touch is too challenging for him.

With Walker, we can look for patterns of covering his ears with loud noises, frequently asking others to be quiet, or avoiding loud places. If these are common occurrences for Walker, we can help him access headphones, help him use words to ask for help, or let others know the sound is too loud. Always keep in mind that bad behavior comes from a place of mean-spirited intent, and regulation comes from a place of self-protection and preservation.

Even when you understand the difference between behavior and dysregulation, most children exhibit both bad behavior and dysregulation. It is the nature of growth and development.

Many factors influence whether your child's behavior is considered bad behavior or dysregulation.

Behavior and regulation are both influenced by being tired, sick, hungry, growth spurts, and environmental changes.

As parents, you are making innumerable game-time decisions about behavior and dysregulation every day. In real time, you are determining whether it is a deliberate behavior or sensory overload. There is no way you can get it right every time. I've never met a parent who is batting a thousand. You are going to make mistakes. Give yourself grace and be kind to yourself. I always say, if you get it right 80% of the time, that is a darn good day. Apologize, ask for forgiveness for the other 20%, and then get on with it. You now have a new tool in your toolbox, a new lens through which to view your child. This is what we want. But, as with anything new, no one comes out of the gate doing it perfectly. Extend yourself grace upon grace, and then get back in the game.

I believe there are very few children who are truly poorly behaved. Many children are dysregulated without being fully equipped to manage their dysregulation. On this premise, let's continue exploring ways we can help our children better care for their sensory systems.

Feed The Need

Eating is a basic need just like sleep, clothing, and shelter. If your child is hungry, you give them food. You feed them. Imagine if your child came to you and said they were hungry, and you responded with, "Honey, if you can try not being hungry for another hour, I'll take you to the park." Or what if your child came to you and said they were cold, and you responded, "If you can stop being cold, I'll go buy you your favorite toy." That sounds crazy, right? No parent would ever do that.

Every time we tell a child who needs to regulate their body with movement to sit still, we are essentially doing that exact thing. A child NEEDS movement to regulate, just like they need food to not feel hungry. So why would we deny a child's need for movement?

We shouldn't. We should feed the need. Regulation comes from feeding their need to move.

Let them move. Encourage them to move. Give them a steady diet of *intentional* movement.

Readiness Comes From Movement—ON REPEAT

It can't be said enough. ***Readiness comes from movement***. Readiness doesn't come from being told to be ready. It doesn't come from watching someone else being regulated, calm, or sitting still. It doesn't come from nagging or belittling. It doesn't come from giving consequences or rewards. These strategies might work for short periods with our tiny people-pleasers—our little ones who hold it together for as long as they can just because they want to please us. But it can't last long-term for them, because their bodies need to move.

It is simply a fact. Readiness comes from movement. And not just any kind of movement. Remember, not all movement is created equal. Our bodies need specific, intentional movement:

> Not all movement is created equal.

Swinging, spinning, and inversion to organize the brain.

Jumping, hopping, stomping, running, pushing, and pulling to calm the body.

And deep pressure throughout the skin and muscles—a hug—to help us feel socially connected to one another.

Hang, hop, hug.

Regulation through movement is how our children ready themselves for the demands of life. But what if those demands are something they just don't want to do? Understanding the impact of preferred versus non-preferred activities on task completion helps us better guide our children as they grow and mature.

Preferred vs. Non-preferred Activities

We all have things we like to do and things we don't—preferred and non-preferred activities. At home, my preferred activities are doing laundry and baking. My non-preferred activities are cleaning and pest control. Preferred and non-preferred activities are a real part of every-one's life. The same is true for our children.

As parents, we are not trying to encourage our children to love everything; we want our children to find their affinities. At the same time, we want to teach them to give the same level of effort and attention to activities they do not enjoy as they do to activities they enjoy. We do this by first acknowledging their preferred and non-preferred activities. In OT, I ask children to tell me something they are really good at in school and something that is hard for them. As mentioned previously, this line of questions lets me see if they can accurately self-assess. It helps me gauge cognitive organization. These questions also give me a window into what they enjoy, where they find success, and their interests.

It is important to fully understand which activities your child prefers and which ones they do not prefer. Don't assume you know. Have a conversation with your child and ask them to rank all their daily activities on a scale of 1-10. One being their absolute least favorite activity and 10 being their most favorite activity. Document their answers for reference when you are planning each day.

When we better understand and acknowledge a child's preferred and non-preferred activities, we are better equipped to anticipate challenges and teach skills to overcome them. I encourage you to adopt the language of preferred and non-preferred activities in your home and share with your children what you like and don't like to do. Find ways to model giving your best effort to tasks you don't prefer, so your children can see firsthand what that looks like in everyday life. Discussing, modeling, and holding each other accountable are great ways to tackle non-preferred activities in your home.

Yes, Transitions ARE Hard

If your child struggles with sensory regulation, it is very likely they also struggle with transitions. Transitions are hard for dysregulated, unreadied children. They don't even know why it's hard, but they know they just can't do what you're asking of them. Three things that make transitions more difficult for children:

- moving from a preferred to a non-preferred activity,

- placing too many additional demands on a child,

- the sensory experience of the transition.

The preferred to non-preferred transition.

When we look at a transition, moving from a preferred activity to a non-preferred activity will always be more difficult. There are three practical steps to support your child.

First, simply acknowledging that you are aware a difficult transition is coming takes much of the pressure off the situation.

Second, ask the child if there is anything that can be done to ease the transition. Do what you can to implement their suggestion. It will give them a sense of control that has been naturally lost in the difficulty of the transition.

Third, use a five-minute notice and a "transition item." The five-minute notice will look like this. A timer will be pre-set to go off five minutes before the preferred activity ends. As your child hears the timer say, "That's our five-minute timer. How would you like to spend these last five minutes?" If they are unable to figure out how to spend the time, you can provide suggestions that typically take five minutes. Examples include coloring one more animal, doing two more passes across the monkey bars, or finding three more words in the puzzle. Once you both agree on how to spend the time, let them work quietly and independently on the agreed-upon task. If they want you involved, then do so, at their request. When the final timer goes off at the end of the five minutes, tell them you will meet them at the door with a transition item. This item could be a balloon, a piece of gum, or a small fidget. You may bring all three and let them choose. The goal of the transition is to keep it calm and predictable, with the transition item providing a small distraction to ease the discomfort. I use the five-minute notice and transition item in the clinic with all the children. I make sure to give them the transition item once they have their shoes on and are walking out the door, to ensure the transition continues on a positive note.

The transition with too many demands and duties.

Another consideration is how many demands or duties we add to the transition. For example, if we are going from home to the car, I might add expectations to pick up your toys, put your dishes in the sink, and not forget your shoes and bookbag. I have single-handedly made the transition more difficult.

I'm going to share a clinic example, because I see this one frequently. When it is time to leave OT (which is usually a preferred to non-preferred transition), I often hear parents give their child a list of directives, in rapid fire, including:

Help clean up! Get the toys you brought! Put the books away! Don't forget your jacket! Tell Ms. Heidi thank you! Give her eye contact when you say goodbye! Tell her you will see her next week! Come back here, face her, and tell her you will see her next week!

Do you see what just happened? We just made it harder by placing additional demands on them. If we are working to improve transitions, we must stay focused on *the transition*. Once we develop a successful routine, we can gradually begin adding the demands and expectations of a more typical transition.

> If we are working to improve transitions, we must stay focused on the transition.

Your child has the skills to pick up their toys, gather their jacket, and say thank you and goodbye, but they are not able to do those things during an already difficult transition. Work on success with simple transitions first, then add in the other demands.

The high sensory demand transition.

The final consideration with a transition is the demand it places on the child's sensory system. When a child is moving from the morning quiet of their bedroom to a bustling kitchen where several people are doing different things, talking in different volumes, eating different foods with various smells, and there is a lot of coming and going, the transition will be far more difficult. This type of change may even send your child into a state of sensory overload or dysregulation.

It's not enough to just understand the sensory aspects of transitions; we must also have tools to alleviate the additional stressors that may be present.

This is especially true when we are leaving a sensory-calm setting and entering a sensory-stimulating one. Sometimes the sensory aspect of the transition is the problem all on its own, and your child's sensory system lets them know. When you and your child realize the sensory demands will be changing dramatically during the transition, it is essential to have a conversation about it in advance. Talk about what it will look and feel like, and prepare tools to help ease the discomfort of an overly stimulating experience. Tools might include bringing headphones, taking a movement break before the transition, or using a code word if things feel too difficult.

What if you are not able to have the conversation in advance? For example, you are going to a birthday party, and as you approach the event, you quickly realize there is a band playing extra loud music, there are far more people than you expected, there is a lot of loud talking, and kids are screaming. We sometimes think we don't have time for the conversation, we might be worried about being late, or we might just feel the child will have to adjust. None of these assumptions usually produces a good result. Instead, stop and talk with your child about how this is different from what they expected. Ask your child if they have any needs or suggestions that might help. They might ask you to stay for a bit while they adjust, or, as mentioned in other scenarios, they may need to use headphones or earplugs. You might develop a code word between the two of you for when your child needs to take a break. You might plan to come back earlier for pickup, since the environment seems quite hectic. Or your child may decide it's just too much, and they won't go. It is okay not to go. Caring for your child's sensory system and allowing them to feel safe and seen is more important than attending the event.

If transitions are challenging and I am working harder than my peers to get through an average day, it makes sense that sleep will also be a struggle. Let's examine sleep hygiene and what we can do to help our children sleep.

Sleep

Saying sleep is essential might be the understatement of all understatements. Getting adequate sleep is vital for all areas of childhood growth and development. Sleep issues can disrupt family dynamics and relationships. When you have concerns about your child's sleep, you want to ask yourself... Are they having difficulty falling asleep? Or are they having difficulty staying asleep? Or both? It is problematic if your child takes longer than 15-20 minutes to *fall asleep*. If your child wakes up with their bed in disarray, their pillow not near their head, their blanket twisted, and their head at the bottom of their bed, they are having restless sleep and an issue *staying asleep*.

Children with regulation issues or who become overstimulated by the demands of the day often have difficulty falling asleep. Their sensory system is overloaded by the day and can't settle into a state of rest. These children will avoid bedtime, become hyperactive right before bed, become hyperverbal, or might even become reckless and disorganized around bedtime. Here is the sleep protocol I prescribe for children whose sleep struggles are related to dysregulation.

- *Acknowledge and recognize that your child's body is having a difficult time shutting down/quieting for the transition to sleep. Do not misunderstand this as sleep avoidance or your child's desire to manipulate a later bedtime. Your child is tired and wants to sleep, just as much as you want them to.*

- *Know that exhaustion in children often looks like hyperactivity. Your child's activity level may increase as fatigue increases. It isn't "a second wind," it is exhaustion. This means you most likely missed the first opportunity to put the child to bed, and now you are trying to help an exhausted child fall asleep.*

Start the bedtime routine/sleep protocol 60 minutes before bedtime.

1. *One hour before bed, turn off TVs, computers, phones, and all screens. Turn the lights down and diffuse lavender. Use lavender as tolerated.*

2. *Also, 60 minutes before bedtime, have your child do 15 minutes of joint pressure activities to help the release of serotonin, which will aid in the transition to sleep. Joint pressure activities include hopping, jumping, running, and playing catch with a weighted ball.*

3. *45 minutes before bed, have your child take a bath/shower and use lavender oils (soap, diffuser, or lotion) as tolerated.*

4. *When your child gets out of the bath/shower, wrap them up tightly with the towel for deep pressure to help calm and settle their bodies. Apply lotion with deep-pressure strokes,*

again to aid in relaxing the body. You may be tempted to tickle your child during these times, but tickling is arousing and should be avoided, as it could prolong the transition to sleep.

5. *Complete teeth brushing, toileting, and the entire bedtime routine with lower light, lower activity level, lower sounds, and calmer voices.*

6. *15 minutes before bedtime, lie in bed with your child and read a calm, rather dull, non-stimulating book quietly together, and let your child lie under a weighted blanket. They may want you to hold them tightly, lie on top of them for a while before bed, or have you wrap them up in blankets. The extra weight helps quiet and calm their bodies in preparation for sleep.*

Your child may need to brain-dump every detail of their day. They are simply trying to clear their brain so they can rest. Let them. When they are brain-dumping, your only response should be to make sounds like, Ohhh, mmmm, uhhh. Don't ask questions, seek clarification, or share info. Save your questions for the next day. This is your child trying to empty their brain, so don't facilitate conversation or stimulate their thoughts. Again, they want to sleep as badly as you want them to, so save the conversation for the morning.

You may adjust the schedule based on your child's individual preferences—e.g., longer bath time, shorter reading time, longer joint pressure time, etc.

This 60-minute routine typically reduces the time to sleep onset almost immediately. Done consistently, it can create a calm, regular sleep routine for your child and your whole family.

If this sleep protocol doesn't produce results, it is recommended that you consult your child's pediatrician and look into other causes of your child's sleep difficulties. Although less common, some children struggle with sleep due to sleep apnea, tonsil and adenoid obstructions, fluid in their ears, or other physiological challenges.

The information in this chapter has given us a framework for better understanding the additional sensory challenges children face. Let's now roll up our sleeves and take a look at our Parenting Toolbox and see what else we need to make it complete.

CHAPTER 10
Your Parenting Toolbox

Congratulations, you have reached the final chapter of this book. Most likely, some of the information was encouraging, some enlightening, and some might have been downright hard to take in and digest. No matter how this information has fallen on your parent heart, I know you have made it to the last chapter because you have a desire to be the best parent you can be to the child(ren) you have been given. That, in and of itself, is admirable and inspiring.

Let's first take a look at the many new tools you have added to your Parenting Toolbox. You have:

- a new lens of sensory regulation
- a social skills assessment
- the sleep protocol
- transition strategies using a transition item
- hang, hop, hug activities
- tools to teach the group membership skills of first-time listening, holding a thought, and unentertained waiting
- tools to teach accurate self-assessment

- a blueprint for a "Put Yourself Back Together" space
- questions to ask if you are looking for a sensory-based OT

Through this process, you might have been inspired to retire some of your less effective tools, such as yelling, impatience, and repeating yourself. Or, you may have moved them to a corner of your Toolbox you rarely visit.

As parents, we are constantly learning and growing. The irony is that just when we feel we have mastered a parenting season, our children go through a growth spurt, and we have to learn a new set of tools all over again. Or even more challenging is having all your children at different developmental stages, requiring you to shift rapidly between developmentally appropriate parenting tools multiple times a day. It can be mind-boggling. As you continue to sort through your Toolbox, remember to extend yourself loads of patience and grace.

Let's explore some more tools that can have a significant impact not only on your parenting but ultimately on the health of your family unit and relationships. Let's start with having an honest conversation about how counterintuitive some of these tools and strategies might feel.

Counterintuitive parenting

There is a portion of parenting that is intuitive. If a child is hungry, you give them food. When a child is tired, you put them down for a nap. If a child is running into traffic, you stop them. These things do not require much frontal lobe function; they are more instinctive. You just know.

Our response to behavior sometimes falls into the category of intuition. If a child does something wrong, they are given a consequence. If they do something right, they are rewarded.

It makes sense. It seems logical.

It is logical because behavior modification is effective at changing behavior and is arguably THE most effective way to do so.

But what if behavior modification doesn't work?

If behavior modification, done correctly, doesn't work, then I challenge you to consider maybe it isn't behavior. Maybe your child is using "behavior" to communicate with you.

I know, I know, this doesn't sit well with everyone. You might even feel a slight tightness in your chest right now. But hear me out.

> Maybe your child is using "behavior" to communicate with you.

Behavior modification is excellent, it just isn't effective for regulation. When a child is dysregulated and letting you know through behavior, behavior modification only addresses the symptom, not the problem. It is like putting a Band-Aid on a cut that needs a suture. You might get short-term relief, but no long-term results.

It will feel counterintuitive when your child "misbehaves," and instead of giving them a consequence, you address their dysregulation.

There is a Seinfeld episode (Season 5, Episode 22) that epitomizes counterintuitive parenting. Throughout the episode, George Costanza comes to realize that if he just does the opposite of his gut instinct, he finds great success in life, and things begin to turn out better for him. This is what it feels like when you begin using your new regulation lens and tools to respond to your child rather than the old behavior modification strategies.

It feels like the opposite.

It feels uncomfortable. But, wow, does it work.

Acknowledging it feels counterintuitive is half the battle; the other half is having strategies to use in the moment. One of my favorite and most impactful tools is Validate and Empower.

Validate and Empower

Validate and empower is one of my favorite non-behavior-modification strategies for responding to your child's dysregulation. Validate and empower is a two-step response to your child's unexpected or unpredictable dysregulation.

The first step is to validate your child. You are not affirming or agreeing with them; you are validating that you see and hear them. Here is what it might look like.

Your child throws a toy across the room.

A behavior modification response would be somewhere along the lines of "We don't throw toys in the house. You might break your toy or hurt someone when you throw toys. If you throw your toy again, I'm going to take it away." The goal of behavior modification is to stop throwing toys. As we already discussed, if it is behavior, this behavior modification approach will achieve the desired outcome. Your child will stop throwing toys. However, if it isn't behavioral in nature, your child will throw whatever they can put their hand on next.

A validation response is, "I see you threw your toy. It seems like you are frustrated. Is that correct?" You are simply acknowledging that you see and hear them, without saying what they are doing is right or wrong. Validation keeps you connected to your child on the path to a solution or resolution. When your child feels seen and heard, they stay connected and will hear you out. Once you have validated your child, take a 3-5 second pause. The power in the pause creates a quiet moment; a space to breathe that usually keeps a meltdown at bay. With this moment of continued connection, you can then move on to step two.

The second step is empowering your child. Empowering is the process of helping them develop an alternative to address their frustration. Empowering is searching for a result, by asking, 1) can you fix it, 2) can I fix it, or 3) can we fix it. In that order. It starts with, "Do you have any ideas how you can let me know you are frustrated?" If they can't come up with something, then you can offer ideas you have used that have worked for you when you've felt frustrated. It might sound something like this, "When I get frustrated, sometimes I go for a walk, or hit my pillow, or go outside and shoot baskets. Do you think any of those options might work for you?" If your suggestion doesn't seem viable to them, then you say, "The two of us are reasonably intelligent people; I bet we can come up with something together." Most of the time, a resolution is found along the journey of, "Can you, can I, can we find a solution?" If a resolution isn't found, it's okay to take a break and come back to the conversation later to find a better option.

Validate and empower is a response that acknowledges you see your child is struggling and tells them you are willing to stay with them to come up with a solution to meet their needs. It allows them to feel supported through their struggle. It says, "I believe you are not a bad kid or ill-intentioned. I understand that you are using behavior to tell me something is challenging or difficult for you. And, I will stay with you and help you come up with a better way."

When we use Validate and Empower instead of behavior modification, we model language for our children that helps them better understand themselves. Language matters. Here are some thoughts on how what we say influences our children's language and their self-perception.

Teaching Children the Language to Use on Themselves

As parents, we've heard it said that the words we speak to children become their inner voice. So if we tell them they are a problem, they believe they are a problem. If we tell them they are defiant and difficult, they believe they are defiant and difficult. If we paint an inaccurate picture of who they are, they will then have an inaccurate self-image.

A child who misunderstands themselves is misunderstood by others.

We must use accurate language to describe our children so they can understand themselves accurately.

Instead of telling a child they are difficult, tell them you can see they are struggling, or that this task is challenging for them.

> We must use accurate language to describe our children so they can understand themselves accurately.

Instead of telling a child they aren't trying hard enough or that everyone else understands it better, tell them you see they are trying and that it is difficult for them.

When a child is hanging upside down off the couch, instead of saying, "We don't hang upside down off the couch," say, "I see you're trying to get your brain organized."

When your child is wiggling all over their chair, instead of saying, "Please sit still!" say, "Your body is telling you it is trying to calm down. Why don't we get up and do some hopping?"

And add, "You know what your body is saying when you do that? It is saying, THANK YOU, THANK YOU, THANK YOU!"

Just by changing your words, you can change how your child views him/herself.

Not only do your words matter, but your own regulation matters. Regulation isn't just a one-man show. Regulation can be transferable. It is called co-regulation, and it is another excellent tool for helping our children. Let's learn more.

Co-regulation

Co-regulation can be defined as "The process through which children develop the ability to soothe and manage distressing emotions and sensations from the beginning of life through connection with nurturing and reliable primary caregivers."[38] I've heard co-regulation oversimplified as using your calm to facilitate your child's calm. I cautiously talk about co-regulation with parents because parent guilt is real (we tackle that next).

Many parents hear co-regulation and think, *Gosh, it is all my fault, my child is dysregulated.* Or, *If only I could keep myself under control, my child wouldn't struggle so badly.* Parent guilt is alive and well for most of us. The world's voice of consumerism even likes to make us feel a little guilty. Consumerism relies on the idea that if you feel bad about what you are doing, you are more likely to purchase items to make you feel better. Effective parenting has no room for parent guilt. It is impossible to perform well from a place of guilt. If you have done something wrong, make it right with an apology and changed behavior, forgive yourself, and get on with it. With that said, if you are dysregulated or become dysregulated in response to your child's dysregulation, Dr. Brooke Weinstein is one of my favorite content writers on co-regulation. She gets it. She produces great content and easy-to-use tools for parents struggling with self-regulation amid their child's dysregulation. You can follow her on Instagram. You can sign up for or join her groups and classes.

---

38 *Co-regulation. Complex Trauma Resources*, 26 Aug. 2020, https://www.complextrauma.org/glossary/co-regulation/. Accessed 30 July 2025.

Did someone say parent guilt?

Parent Guilt

You have heard the saying, *If you are worried about being a good parent, you already are one.* If you are concerned with the quality of your parenting or thinking about what type of parent you are, you are already being intentional and working to be your best.

Just sit with that for a moment.

Along with wanting to do right by your children comes guilt when you don't do things well.

Here is a short list of things parents feel guilty about:

Stay-at-home parents feel guilty about not getting their kids out more with other kids.

Employed parents feel guilty about not spending more time with their children.

Most parents feel guilty about not providing more for their children.

Some parents feel guilty about the school their children go to.

Some parents feel guilty about not seeing the obvious sooner.

Some parents feel guilty about giving their kids too much screen time.

The list goes on and on...

If there is one thing that will make your energy more efficient, it is curbing the energy you spend on parent guilt.

Parent guilt is wasted energy.

None of us has extra energy to expend, and in all honesty, most of us are trying to figure out how to conserve energy just to make it through each day. The best energy conservation strategy I recommend is to ditch the parent guilt. If you spend more than two minutes feeling guilty, it's too long. Within those two minutes, you can apologize for the thing you did wrong, move on, and do better the next time. There are no expert parents; there are just parents doing their very best with what they have.

> There are no expert parents; there are just parents doing their very best with what they have.

You are doing the very best with what you have. Period.

You are reading this book and equipping yourself with new tools, for heaven's sake!

You are aspiring to do better every day.

No shame, no guilt.

Now, what if more than one person is helping raise your child? Some children are growing up in two households, while others have a nanny or au pair in their home. Some households include grandparents. If there are more than two adults involved in the upbringing of your child(ren), here are some valuable considerations to keep in mind.

Nannies and Multi-home Families

** The information in this section **excludes** concerns about physical, emotional, or sexual harm to a child. Such concerns should be referred to and handled immediately by the appropriate professionals and officials.*

Simply put, having an additional childcare provider in your home, whether it be a nanny, au pair, grandparents, or long-term babysitter, adds a third "parent" to the mix. This also applies to multi-home families of divorce, separation, or multi-generational arrangements.

Having more than one or two parents involved is a complicating factor.

In most families, it is challenging enough to get two parents on the same page with parenting styles and goals. When you bring in another childcare provider, there are many things to consider.

- Does the third or additional childcare provider share your same parenting perspectives and goals?

- Who will be taking the lead on discipline? Do all adults have permission to discipline in the same way?

- What tools do they have in their Toolbox, and which tools are their go-tos?

- Do they have an understanding of regulation? If so, what is it?

The reason this topic is even included in this book is that I have seen families unravel at the expense of the child when their adults are not on the same page. Children are savvy, and they can easily pick up on who they can do what with. Which parent they can whine to and which one they can be silly with. Which parent is soft and easy to manipulate, and which parent stands firm on their word.

With families who have more than two parents, I like to have them do this simple activity together.

Have each childcare provider make a list of what they like about the others' parenting styles. Review the lists, then pick a few items that everyone agrees to integrate into their own Parenting Toolbox. Many multi-parent families focus on what the other parents/caregivers are doing wrong or poorly, and then hang their hat on that one concern, and put it on repeat. "If they would just stop doing that one thing, everything would be better for my child."

This is a problem-based approach.

I recommend a strengths-based approach where we focus on what the other parents are doing well, integrate that into our Toolbox, and use it more often to provide consistency and predictability for the child.

The one thing every parent/caregiver has in common is that they want what is best for their child.

As much as what another parent is doing may be annoying to you, if you can look at them as someone who deeply loves your child and who also only wants what is best for them, then it is easier to get on the same page. This only helps your child and provides a more predictable and emotionally safe environment for them. In a predictable and secure environment, a child can thrive and grow to reach their full potential.

Once we get everyone on the same parenting page and have the family unit heading down the right path, coming up with a family motto is a meaningful family activity.

> In a predictable and secure environment, a child can thrive and grow to reach their full potential.

A Family Motto

A family motto is a way to solidify your family's identity. It helps unify the family unit and enables family members to easily recognize what they have in common. Some of my favorite family mottos are:

We Do Hard Things

We Love Deeply

We Forgive

We Show Gratitude

We Try New Things

We Give Back

Hold a family meeting and discuss what your family stands for. What do you want others to see when they meet your family? What is the purpose of your family? Then, agree upon a Family Motto. Print it up. Frame it. Put it around the house.

Families are ever-changing. It is okay to update or change your family motto every few years as your family changes and transforms. Have fun with it.

So, that's *The Readied Child* in a nutshell.

Well, not exactly. Truthfully, this is just the beginning. It's a framework that works for families. I have seen it work time and time again over my 35 years in Occupational Therapy.

With your new lens, it becomes easier to understand your child more accurately. Changing the lens through which you view your child and using the information and tools from this book not only helps transform your child but also your relationship *with* your child.

With these new and powerful tools in your Parenting Toolbox, you are better equipped to help your child be ready to learn and ultimately ready for life. I believe that you, as a parent, can do this. You are enough. You are perfectly designed for your child. You are fully equipped. Everything is going to be okay.

The tools in this book are for now, but they are also for later. You will find them relevant throughout all phases of your parenting journey.

Philippians 4:8 is a Bible verse I frequently reflect on. I share it in hopes that you can find what is *true, noble, right, pure, lovely, admirable, excellent, and praiseworthy* every step of the way along your journey.

Parenting Tools
Quick Reference

Tool	Chapter	Page
Accurate Self Assessment - Independent Self Advocacy - Launch	2	37
Animal Walks	5	84
Bats and Butterflies	4	65
Behavior v Regulation	9	137
Blanket Swing	4	71
Burrito Wrap	6	99
Car Sickness	7	108
Chair Push-Ups	5	81
Child Language	10	156
Co-Regulation	10	157
Common Signs of Disorganization, Excitability, and Disconnection	7	106
Counterintuitive Parenting	10	152
Family Motto	10	161
Family Sandwich	6	98
Feed the Need	9	140
Fight or Flight	7	111
Filing Cabinet v Cardboard Box	4	56
Finding a Sensory OT	7	115
First Time Listener	8	119
Front Rolls	4	68
FUF Crashes	6	102
Hang - Hop - Hug	7	109

Suggested Reading

Sensory

Understanding Your Child's Sensory Signals by Angie Voss

Sensory Integration and the Child by A. Jean Ayres

Executive Functioning

Smart but Scattered by Peg Dawson and Richard Guare

Social Skills

Super Skills by Judith Coucouvanis

Childhood Development

Yardsticks by Chip Wood

Author Bio

Heidi Tringali is a dedicated pediatric occupational therapist, an inspiring speaker, and a proud mother of two adult children. With degrees in Special Education and Psychology from Hastings College, an Occupational Therapy degree from Tufts University, and over 30 years of experience as an Occupational Therapist, she has developed a passion for supporting children and their families.

In 2006, Heidi founded Tringali Occupational Therapy Services (T.O.T.S.), which empowers schools and preschools nationwide through training and consultative services. She offers professional development for educators and meaningful training for families on key topics, including learning readiness, classroom success, and unlocking each child's potential.

As a member of the American Occupational Therapy Association (AOTA), Heidi serves as a media expert, raising awareness and understanding of pediatric occupational therapy. She also serves as an expert witness and consultant in legal matters in this field. Additionally, she is certified by the National Board for Certification in Occupational Therapy (NBCOT).

Heidi lives in Charlotte, NC, with her husband, Tony. You can contact her at HeidiTringali.com or CharlotteOT.com.